World Building Guide & Workbook

TG Franklin

PROJECT TITLE

Introduction

Several years ago, I wrote *Fundamentals of World Building* (under a pseudonym), designed as an informational guide for the beginning world builder. Due to the passing of one of the partners, the publisher of *Fundamentals* went out of business in 2013, and the rights reverted back to me. I saw this as an opportunity to expand on the original premise and take *Fundamentals* out of the information for beginners stage to something more.

Most of the original work remains, but it has been expanded.

Still, let's start with the basics.

Before You Begin: The Story Bible

Some writers keep a story world notebook, commonly referred to as a bible, to keep track of their world elements. While this workbook will serve the purpose well for most of your world building information, if you have research materials, articles, or photos, I strongly recommend that you invest in a separate story bible.

There are several options available, whether you prefer hard copy or electronic storage.

A spiral bound notebook: purchase one that has dividers, such as a five-subject notebook, to keep your information organized.

A three-ring binder with dividers, preferably with pockets, or letter-sized manila folders: I have found the folders work well if you want to remove one portion of the information and work on it without the clumsiness of a notebook. Labels can include characters (major and minor), places, transportation, clothing, magic spells, maps, rituals, plot points, secrets, or anything the writer deems important about the story world. Color folders are also available for color-coding.

Pocket dividers can hold bits of information you acquire from magazine or newspaper articles or the Internet, as well as photographs, maps, or ideas scribbled on a napkin during lunch. Sheet protectors are also a good idea if you plan on using full-page articles, maps, or large photographs, as they will protect those items from being lost, stained, or torn.

Of course, pocket dividers, sheet protectors, and pouches (for pens and holding note and idea cards) can be used with the folder method. Use whatever works and fits with your writing style.

Another route, if you're comfortable with having the information on the Internet as opposed to hard copy, is to create your own world-building wiki. Several websites offer free wikis. Some even have a wiki that will transfer to a hard drive or a USB drive for portability. Wikis are a good place to store a lot of information. In any search engine, type the words, "free wiki." A list of several sites will be at your fingertips. Be sure to check them out thoroughly and choose one that best fits your needs. If you want to have parts of your wiki private and parts of it public, be certain you can create both public and private pages before you start adding information.

There are also several apps available to store notes, articles, and photos. And no matter how you keep your story world information organized, make copies and backups.

What is world building?

World building is so much more than creating a planet in a galaxy far, far away. It's more than setting. It's more than mood, tone, and exotic elements. It's more than language.

It's taking the foreign, the alien, and the unfamiliar, and making it resonate with readers. Readers should not feel like an outsider or a spectator of the world. They need to identify with the characters, whether those characters are humanoid, demon, angel, vampire, were, or an alien form of life.

Simply stated, the writer must make the unbelievable believable.

In the world of speculative fiction, it's not only important to have a great story, it's imperative to have a great story world.

What is a Story World?

In the most simple terms, the story world is the setting in which the story takes place, whether it be outer space, a lost city such as Atlantis, or an alternate or parallel universe. However, setting is the broad stroke of the brush, the background for the details that bring the story to life.

Clothing, food and drink, architecture, weather, terrain, vehicles, furniture, types of energy, and art are only a few of the minute details that will decorate the story world.

A thinly veiled version of life on Earth, either from the 12th century or the current century, will read exactly like what it is—an amateurish attempt. No matter how well the author has crafted the plot, if the story world doesn't enhance the story to its fullest potential, the story falls flat.

The story world must be as fully developed as the characters and the plot. Even a world of chaos must be structured and fleshed out in such a way that the reader can relate and fully immerse himself in the world. Readers need to feel at home in the story world, whether it's another planet or another dimension.

Balance is the key. The story world should not overwhelm the story. Nor should it linger around the edges of the story, creeping in only when needed to explain a story element. Story and story world should be an intricately woven tapestry, each thread dependent on the other to present the whole pattern. Any bare spot, any frayed edge, any torn or faded thread will ruin the aesthetic value of the art.

To build a story world, the author must be part artist, part engineer, and sometimes part mad scientist. Elements need to be built and structured with the greatest attention to detail and then painted with the visionary's palette.

It's hard work and, like any building project, it requires blueprints or instructions and the proper tools.

This workbook is not intended to be a complete reference, a compendium of world-building knowledge, or even how to write a speculative fiction novel. It is drawing the blueprint for the construction of a story world, the elements that comprise the different types of world, and how those elements interact to create a believable story world.

Where to Start?

Every writer has their own unique process. Don't feel like you must build your story world in the same way as the steps are presented in this workbook. In fact, you'll probably do a lot of flipping back and forth.

If your story idea starts with a situation, go ahead and pull the story world elements out of it and add them to the workbook as they appear.

If you enjoy mapping out all of the locations before writing any of the story, feel free to draw the maps and locations first.

If you want to create your magic systems or technology first, feel free to do so.

There's no right or wrong way to start.

The sequence presented in this workbook is my preferred method — with some overlap.

The first worksheet is designed as an overview. A blueprint, of sorts, to jot down initial thoughts and ideas for later expansion. It isn't necessary to know or have all of this information at the beginning.

Just as a construction crew wouldn't start to build a house without a set of blueprints, an author shouldn't try to build a story world without them. Each blueprint in the set will contain the basic shape and size of the building. One blueprint will have the foundation specifications, one will have the interior walls, doors, and windows marked. One blueprint will have the electrical diagrams, and another will have plumbing diagrams. To build a story world, the writer needs a full set of blueprints.

The writer is the architect of the story and therefore is also the creator of the blueprints.

One of my father's maxims was, "Pencils are made for remembering." If I don't write something down, I will invariably forget it. The same holds true for story world details.

The blueprints may encompass the whole of the story world, or one set of blueprints may be created for a city, state, or region. The story world may require several sets of blueprints, depending on the number of physical locations in the story and the number of different societies. However, don't let the idea of creating several sets of blueprints become intimidating.

I recommend building from the smallest story world to the universal story world. If the story is a space epic, the task of fitting smaller worlds, such as several different planets, into a universe that has already been fully fleshed out and built is harder than structuring the universe around the smaller worlds.

The sections of the world-building worksheet correspond to the different blueprints and expanded further in this workbook. Not all of the information asked for on the worksheet will need to be used in the story. However, the information is necessary for the writer to develop a clear vision of the story world and to relate the vision into words.

The Landscape:

What type of world is being built? (e.g. time travel, fantasy, space opera, etc.)

Fantasy

What is the tone, mood, atmosphere, of the World? (e.g. dystopian, utopian, etc.)

_____

Will it encompass a universe, a country, a region, a city, or a neighborhood?

Several kingdoms/regions - maybe also countries

The Foundation:

What length is the story (short story, novella, novel)? _Novel_

Mythology of the world:

How was the world created/formed? _____

_____

_____

Have there been any major wars, plagues, natural disasters, etc, that have had an impact on

the society, its growth, or evolution so that the effects are inherent to the story?

_____

_____

_____

The Floors, Walls, & Roof:

Will the government be a major factor in this story? _____

(If you're unsure of genre, government, or economic system, the listed examples are explained simply in the indexes.) If so, what is the core model of the government?

☒ Monarchy	☒ Dictatorship
☒ Democracy	☒ Socialism
☒ Republic	☒ Feudalism
☒ Communism	☒ Totalitarianism
☒ Theocracy	☒ Tribal/Clan
☒ Oligarchy	☒ Anarchy

Other (describe) _____

Does the government control trade? _____

What is the government's war policy? _____

_____

What is the government's diplomacy policy? _____

Have embassies been built? _____

Are there secret police or other secret government agencies? _____

Is there a spy network? _____

Does the government control births, deaths, marriages? _____

If so, what are the criteria? _____

_____

How does the court system work? _____

Will the military play a role in the story? _____

Briefly describe the hierarchy of the military, the different branches, how the military is

compensated, how advancement within the ranks is achieved, and any laws that only relate

to military personnel. _____

_____

_____

_____

_____

The Electrical/Plumbing/Heating & Air:

Does religion play a vital or pivotal role in the story? _____

Is there a central religion, state religion, or religious freedom? _____

Briefly describe the religion(s): _____

_____

_____

_____

_____

What type of economic system(s) does the world have?

- ☒ Capitalist
- ☒ Free Market
- ☒ Planned
- ☒ Spoils of War
- ☒ Tribute
- ☒ Barter
- ☒ Corporate Owned
- ☒ None (Anarchy

Other (describe): _____

_____

What type(s) of currency is/are used? _____

What type of educational system does the world have?

- ☒ Free to All
- ☒ Government controlled
- ☒ Religion controlled
- ☒ Only to the rich
- ☒ Only to royalty
- ☒ Only to religious leaders
- ☒ Private Institutions only
- ☒ Specialized (testing for math, science, etc., to determine education)
- ☒ Through apprenticeship, indentured servitude, etc..
- ☒ None

Other (describe): _____

_____

_____

Taboos, superstitions, and traditions that have developed from government mandate, religious mandate, or lack of education: _____

_____

_____

Holidays, feast days, or observances that have developed from government mandate, religious mandate, or other: _____

_____

_____

The Doors & Windows:

What technologies have developed? _____

_____

_____

What technologies are needed (but not yet developed)? _____

_____

_____

Are any technologies banned or outlawed? Why? _____

_____

_____

What types of magic are present? _____

_____

_____

What spells or abilities are needed? _____

_____

_____

Are any magical abilities banned or outlawed? Why? _____

_____

_____

Remembering story tone and theme, what types of art are permitted? _____

_____

_____

Remembering story tone and theme, what types of art are not permitted? Why? _____

_____

Are there any great artists, philosophers, prophets, or leaders (past or present) who have had

an impact on the world? _____

_____

The Rooms: Class Segments: A list for your reference.

- ☑ Royal
- ☑ government workers
- ☑ politicians
- ☑ aristocracy
- ☑ scientific
- ☑ religious
- ☑ medical
- ☑ educators
- ☑ administration (private industry)
- ☑ banking
- ☑ business/shop keepers
- ☑ military
- ☑ law enforcement
- ☑ criminal
- ☑ factory workers
- ☑ celebrities
- ☑ artists
- ☑ sports/athletes
- ☑ farmers/food producers
- ☑ laborers
- ☑ servant/service industry
- ☑ laborers
- ☑ slaves
- ☑ civil servants (garbage workers, maintenance workers, etc.)

Specialized Segments:

- ☑ wizards/witches
- ☑ fairies
- ☑ weres
- ☑ vampires
- ☑ dragons/centaurs/other creatures
- ☑ shapeshifters
- ☑ psychics
- ☑ symbiotes
- ☑ Other _____
- ☑ demons
- ☑ angels
- ☑ aliens
- ☑ gods & goddesses
- ☑ ghosts/spirits
- ☑ robots/androids
- ☑ super heroes/villains
- ☑ mages

The Geography:

Remembering the tone and theme of the world, write a brief description of the physical landscapes that will be used in this world. Include roadways, bodies of water, space/sky, architecture, sacred buildings, graveyards, plants, animals, colors, textures, temperatures, smells, etc. _____

_____

_____

_____

_____

_____

_____

What are the modes of travel? _____

_____

_____

_____

The Decorations:

Remembering story tone & theme, and what types of technology, magic, and art are allowed/banned, describe the following: (for example, in a theocracy, it may be that only religious symbols can be used for decoration on public buildings, or even in private homes.)
Clothing, Hairstyles, jewelry: _____

_____

_____

Food & drink (include delicacies, aphrodisiacs, alcohol, forbidden, poisonous, etc.):

_____

_____

_____

_____

Architecture: _____

_____

_____

_____

Domestic animals/pets: _____

_____

_____

_____

Furniture: _____

_____

_____

_____

Weapons: _____

_____

_____

_____

Tools: _____

_____

_____

_____

Music, writings, paintings: _____

_____

_____

Mystical objects: _____

_____

_____

_____

Drugs (legal & illegal): _____

_____

_____

_____

Crimes: _____

_____

_____

_____

Sports & games: _____

_____

_____

_____

It All Starts With Character

Here's why I prefer to start with the main characters:

In masonry, the cornerstone is the first, and most important, stone laid for a building. It serves as a guide for the placement and position of the rest of the structure and is a connecting point. The cornerstone of the story world is/are the main character(s). The main characters may be hero and heroine, hero/heroine and mentor, best friends, or mortal enemies. Everything else in the story world will relate to the cornerstone and be built in reference to the main characters and their relationships with each other. The characters connect the reader to the story and story world.

The importance of the cornerstone character to the story world is paramount. Think about some of the characters who have stood out in the books and movies you have on your keeper shelf. One thing they all have in common is their passionate belief, even when the first glimpse of their worlds contradicts their convictions. Readers connect with characters who believe the aliens are hostile when the aliens haven't shown any violent behavior, or the time traveler who believes he can change things for the better, or the character who knows he can find the lost city, the treasure, or the cure. Readers connect and root for the main characters because of the character's unfailing, passionate belief.

The idea of a strong cornerstone is also true from an intellectual standpoint. *Primum non nocere* (First, do no harm) can be considered the cornerstone of medicine. This sort of cornerstone idea can be related to the main character in the form of story theme. If the theme is revenge, the world builder needs to know why the character is seeking revenge. Then the builder must determine what in the story world will provide the opportunities to accomplish the goal, or present obstacles to keep the main character from obtaining the goal, and thus provide growth and conflict for the character. The obstacles could be physical, such as long distances, impassable mountains, etc., or they could be ideologies of the society such as the belief that obtaining revenge will bring sorrow to the avenger's family for seven generations, and the character will be forced to live through all seven generations and witness all of the sorrow he caused.

These are all parts of the weaving process the writer must learn to accomplish with ease. Using the physical story world to enhance the story's tone, theme, and plot, or the character's goal, motivation, and conflict is what makes the great stories memorable.

Creating the main characters first also ensures an organic relationship between the characters and the world. After all, we're building the world for our characters, and they will spend their lives in the worlds we create. They will live, love, hate, laugh, regret, journey, and die there.

Every character lives in their own world. The landscape may be the same, but they will each see and experience it through the filter of their individual points of view.

First, determine who's story you're telling. There is probably more than one main character in the story, and each character will have their own story arc. At this point, you may choose to start developing your main characters, just the protagonist and antagonist, or all of your primary and secondary characters, depending on the length of the project and how much time you want to invest in the characters in this early stage. If you already have an idea of your plot, and the idea involves a romantic arc between two main characters, or if there is a clear hero and villain, I recommend initial development of those characters now so the physical journey through their world will mirror, complement, or conflict with their emotional journey as needed.

List your characters & when you expect them to enter your story:

Main Character: _____
Main Character: _____
Main Character: _____
Main Character: _____
Main Character: _____

Secondary Character: _____
Secondary Character: _____
Secondary Character: _____
Secondary Character: _____
Secondary Character: _____
Secondary Character: _____

Tertiary Character: _____
Tertiary Character: _____
Tertiary Character: _____
Tertiary Character: _____
Tertiary Character: _____
Tertiary Character: _____

Notes: (character relationships, etc.)

_____

_____

_____

_____

_____

_____

_____

_____

_____

_____

_____

_____

_____

Character Worksheet

Character:

Description:

What he/ she cares deeply about		Leads to: →

Skills Abilities Strengths Education		Leads to: →

Fears Secrets		Leads to: →

GOALS MOTIVATIONS CONFLICT

```
┌─────────────────────────┐   Notes, quirks, clothing, relationships:
│                         │   _____
│     (pic or drawing)    │   _____
│                         │   _____
│                         │   _____
│                         │   _____
│                         │   _____
│                         │   _____
│                         │   _____
└─────────────────────────┘
```

_____

_____

_____

_____

_____

_____

_____

_____

_____

_____

_____

_____

_____

_____

_____

_____

_____

CHARACTER WORKSHEET

Character:

Description:

What he/she cares deeply about		Leads to: →	GOALS MOTIVATIONS CONFLICT	
Skills Abilities Strengths Education		Leads to: →		
Fears Secrets		Leads to: →		

	Notes, quirks, clothing, relationships:
(pic or drawing)	_____
	_____
	_____
	_____
	_____
	_____
	_____

_____

_____

_____

_____

_____

_____

_____

_____

_____

_____

_____

_____

_____

_____

_____

Character Worksheet

Character:

Description:

What he/she cares deeply about		Leads to:

Skills Abilities Strengths Education		Leads to:

Fears Secrets		Leads to:

GOALS MOTIVATIONS CONFLICT

```
┌─────────────────────────────┐   Notes, quirks, clothing, relationships:
│                             │   _____
│      (pic or drawing)       │   _____
│                             │   _____
│                             │   _____
│                             │   _____
│                             │   _____
│                             │   _____
│                             │   _____
└─────────────────────────────┘
_____
_____
_____
_____
_____
_____
_____
_____
_____
_____
_____
_____
_____
_____
_____
_____
```

Character Worksheet

Character:

Description:

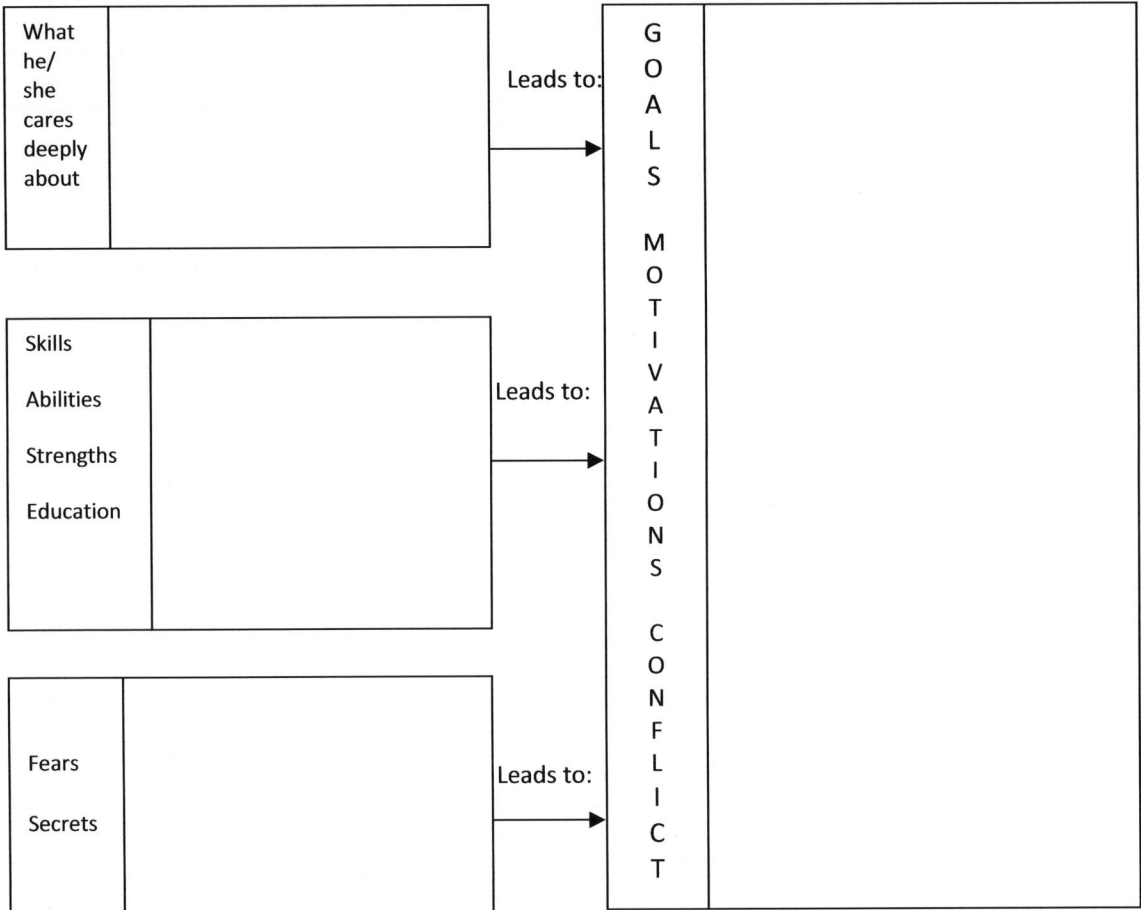

What he/she cares deeply about		Leads to:	GOALS MOTIVATIONS CONFLICT
Skills Abilities Strengths Education		Leads to:	
Fears Secrets		Leads to:	

(pic or drawing)

Notes, quirks, clothing, relationships:

_____

_____

_____

_____

_____

_____

_____

_____

_____

_____

_____

_____

_____

_____

_____

_____

_____

_____

_____

_____

_____

_____

_____

_____

Character Worksheet

Character:

Description:

What he/ she cares deeply about	

Leads to: →

| Skills

Abilities

Strengths

Education	

Leads to: →

| Fears

Secrets	

Leads to: →

GOALS MOTIVATIONS CONFLICT

```
(pic or drawing)
```

Notes, quirks, clothing, relationships:

_____

_____

_____

_____

_____

_____

_____

_____

_____

_____

_____

_____

_____

_____

_____

_____

_____

_____

_____

_____

_____

_____

_____

_____

CHARACTER WORKSHEET

Character:

Description:

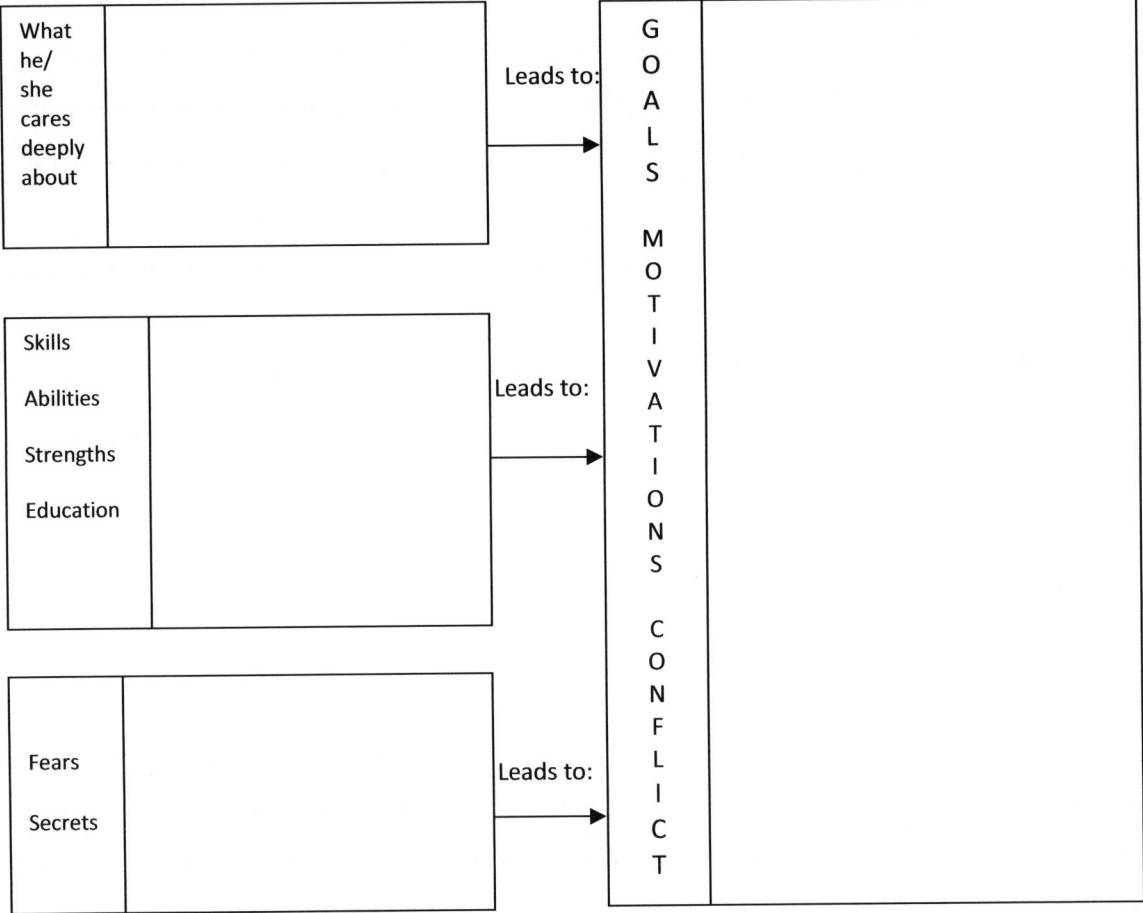

What he/ she cares deeply about		Leads to:	G O A L S M O T I V A T I O N S C O N F L I C T	
Skills Abilities Strengths Education		Leads to:		
Fears Secrets		Leads to:		

(pic or drawing)

Notes, quirks, clothing, relationships:

_____
_____
_____
_____
_____
_____
_____

_____
_____
_____
_____
_____
_____
_____
_____
_____
_____
_____
_____
_____
_____
_____
_____
_____

CHARACTER WORKSHEET

Character:

Description:

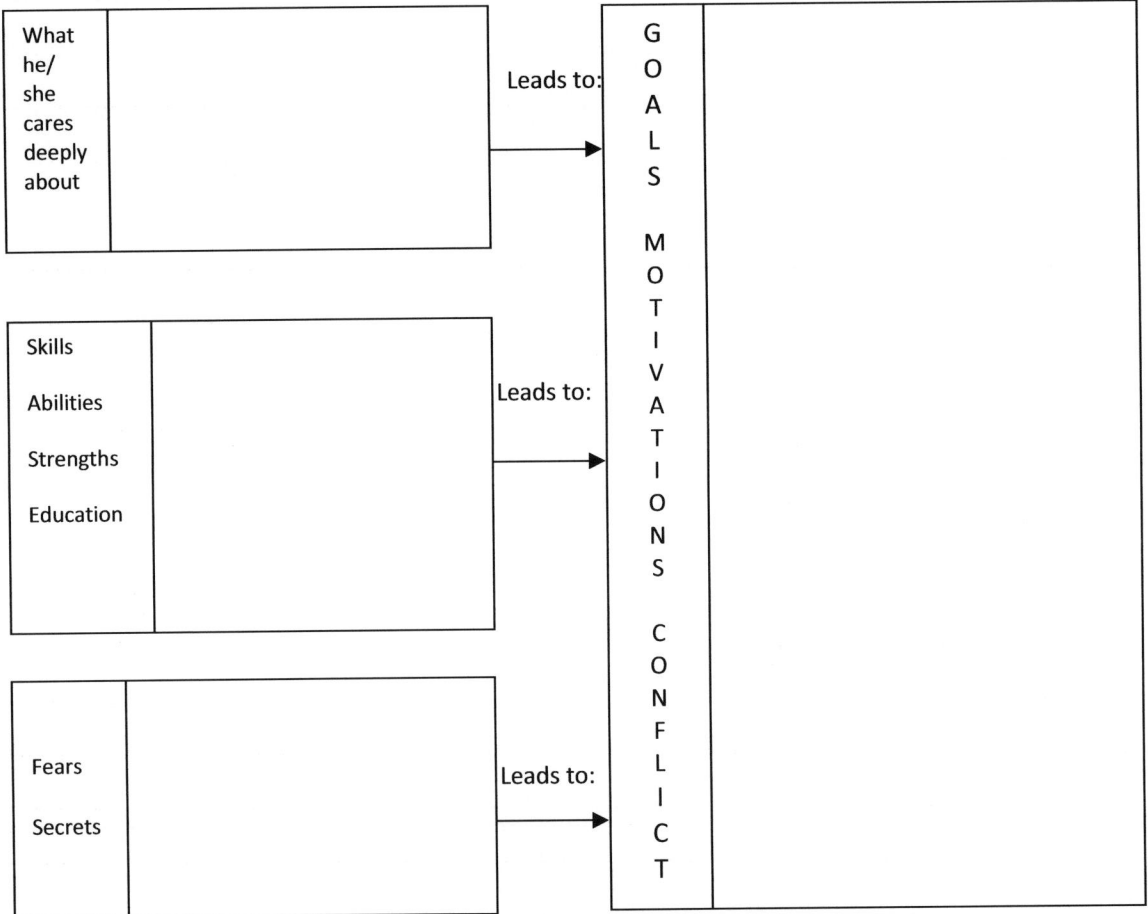

(pic or drawing)	Notes, quirks, clothing, relationships:
	_____
	_____
	_____
	_____
	_____
	_____
	_____
	_____

_____

_____

_____

_____

_____

_____

_____

_____

_____

_____

_____

_____

_____

_____

_____

_____

_____

_____

Character Worksheet

Character:

Description:

What he/ she cares deeply about		Leads to:		GOALS MOTIVATIONS CONFLICT
Skills Abilities Strengths Education		Leads to:		
Fears Secrets		Leads to:		

```
┌─────────────────────────┐   Notes, quirks, clothing, relationships:
│                         │   _____
│     (pic or drawing)    │   _____
│                         │   _____
│                         │   _____
│                         │   _____
│                         │   _____
│                         │   _____
│                         │   _____
│                         │   _____
└─────────────────────────┘   _____
```

_____

_____

_____

_____

_____

_____

_____

_____

_____

_____

_____

_____

_____

_____

_____

_____

_____

_____

Character Worksheet

Character:

Description:

What he/ she cares deeply about		Leads to:

Skills Abilities Strengths Education		Leads to:

Fears Secrets		Leads to:

GOALS MOTIVATIONS CONFLICT

```
┌─────────────────────┐   Notes, quirks, clothing, relationships:
│                     │   _____
│   (pic or drawing)  │   _____
│                     │   _____
│                     │   _____
│                     │   _____
│                     │   _____
│                     │   _____
│                     │   _____
└─────────────────────┘   _____
```

_____

_____

_____

_____

_____

_____

_____

_____

_____

_____

_____

_____

_____

_____

Character Worksheet

Character:

Description:

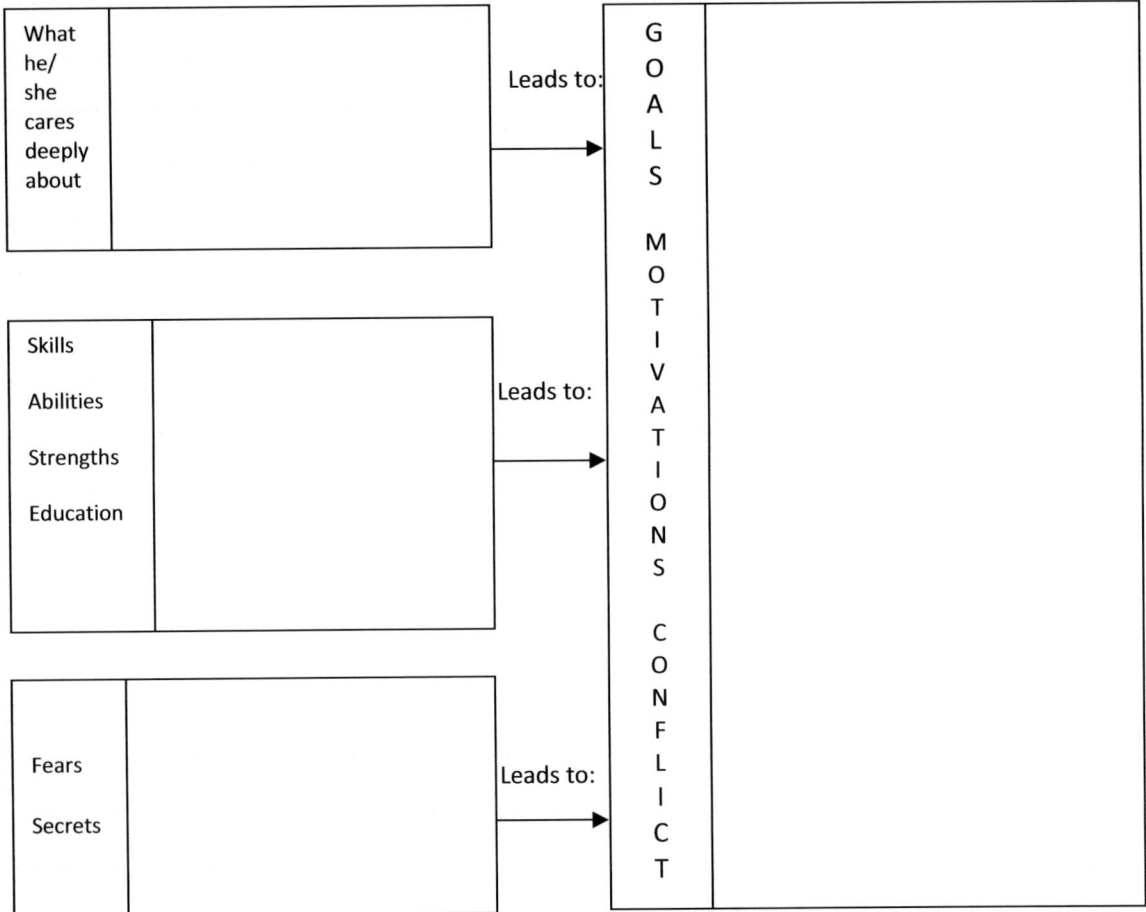

What he/she cares deeply about		Leads to: →
Skills Abilities Strengths Education		Leads to: →
Fears Secrets		Leads to: →

GOALS MOTIVATIONS CONFLICT

(pic or drawing)

Notes, quirks, clothing, relationships:

_____

_____

_____

_____

_____

_____

_____

_____

_____

_____

_____

_____

_____

_____

_____

_____

_____

_____

_____

_____

_____

_____

_____

_____

Character Worksheet

Character:

Description:

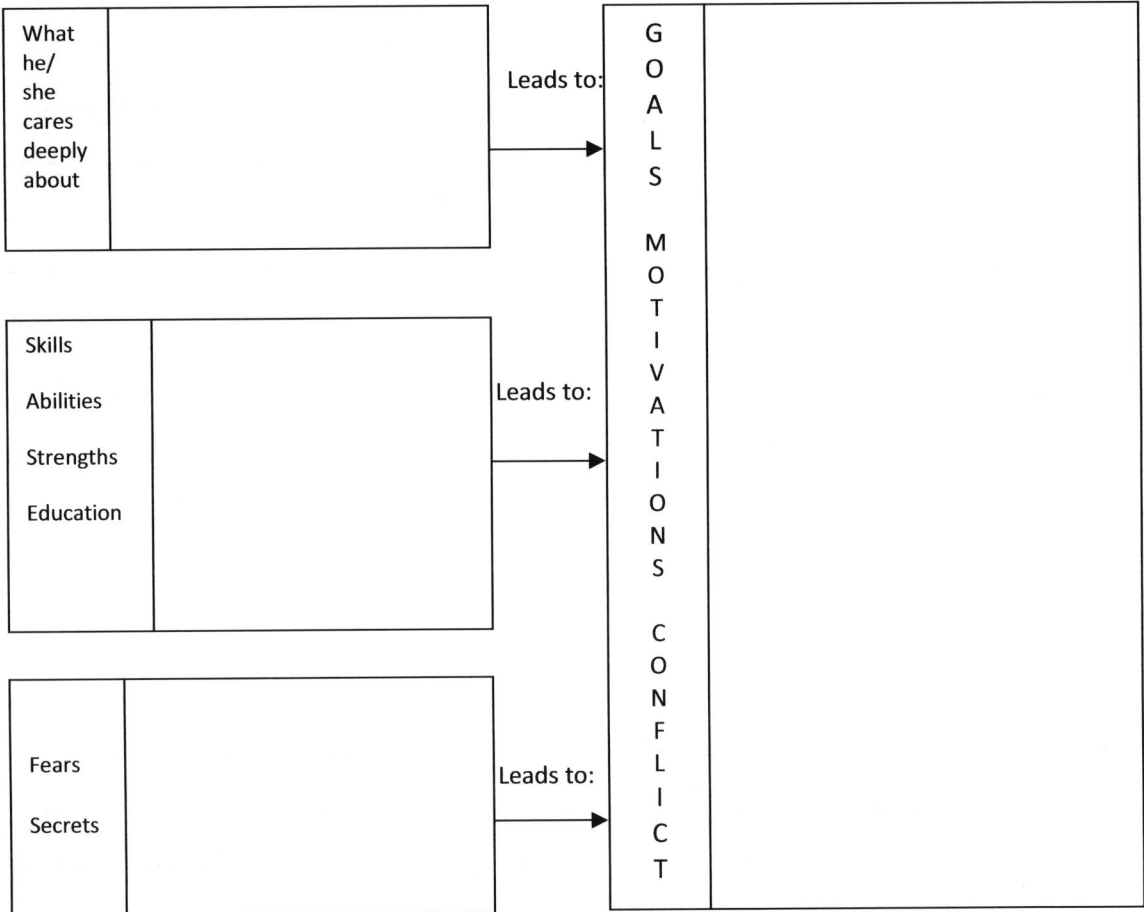

What he/ she cares deeply about		Leads to:	G O A L S M O T I V A T I O N S C O N F L I C T	
Skills Abilities Strengths Education		Leads to:		
Fears Secrets		Leads to:		

```
┌─────────────────────────────┐   Notes, quirks, clothing, relationships:
│                             │   _____
│      (pic or drawing)       │   _____
│                             │   _____
│                             │   _____
│                             │   _____
│                             │   _____
│                             │   _____
│                             │   _____
└─────────────────────────────┘
```

Pick a World, Any World

The Landscape:

The landscape for a speculative fiction world is not limited to science fiction, space opera, high fantasy, or urban fantasy. Do you want to write mysteries? Thrillers? Romance? Westerns? Any genre and any time period is possible in speculative fiction.

Some (lucky) writers know they want to write sword and sorcery, or sweeping starship battles, or super heroes, others want to write to the market (which is fine), and others want to write only for themselves (also fine). However, if you're not sure where you want to start, or if you're interested in experimenting, but not in trial and error, look at your favorite stories, no matter the medium, and look for commonalities, such as themes, a certain type of character, or a specific location or era. This isn't a new idea. It's an exercise that's been around for years to help authors find their voice and writing paths.

- A recurring theme might be coming of age, love conquers all, circle of life, overcoming fear, or quest.
- A recurring character archetype might be the orphan, the explorer, the caregiver, or the rebel.
- A recurring era or location might be Regency, Victorian, Old West, outer space, US, London, or feudal Japan.

Take a moment and list the commonalities. As an example, my list from my favorite books and movies looks like this:

Reluctant heroes
Police procedurals - quest
Urban fantasy - good v. evil, love conquers all, quest
Futuristic, or futuristic feel
Small, core group
Technology gone wrong
Space opera - good v. evil, quest

Looking at my list, it isn't hard to see what I'm drawn to: the classic reluctant hero, forced to go on a quest with a small group of friends, in a futuristic setting, and my main character may or may not find love. I wasted almost ten years of my writing life penning other types of stories. Those stories were serviceable, but they lacked something. When I began writing stories that hit the points on my list, I discovered what my earlier stories were missing — the spark and passion of my authorial voice. And once I found my voice, my stories started to shine.

Now, looking at your list, what are the elements that you think would strengthen your authorial voice?

_____

_____

_____

_____

_____

Take a look at Appendix A – Types of Story Worlds and read the descriptions. Do any of them fit with your authorial voice? I'm guessing several of them do.

Side Note: Over the years, I've heard that time-travel is dead, that editors hate alternate dimension stories, that the vampire/dystopian/whatever market is saturated. I've heard that readers want long, epic reads instead of novellas or short stories. Or, that shorter novels are now selling better due to our fast-paced society. Or, that trilogies are the preferred series length instead of a sweeping, fifteen book saga. Don't listen to anyone about your story. Write the story you are passionate about.

What type of story world appeals to you based on your authorial voice? Why? And keep the following in mind:

    ☑ How much research are you willing to do?
    ☑ Are you planning on writing a standalone story? A trilogy? A series?
    ☑ Is the market over/under saturated in one of the genres?
    ☑ Can you give your story something fresh or unique to make it stand out?

_____

_____

_____

Once you have it narrowed down, start with the broad strokes. Clichés even. There's a reason steampunk stories have gears and brass goggles, and that fantasy stories have magic, and often, fantastical creatures. Each genre and sub-genre has it's own tropes. They help to ground the reader in the story world. Remember, however, that you can't just slap a pair of brass goggles on a character and call it a steampunk, or give a character a computer and call it cyberpunk.

List a few of the broad strokes of your story world landscape:

_____

_____

_____

_____

_____

_____

And list a few of the details and flourishes that will make it uniquely your story world:

_____

_____

_____

_____

_____

_____

_____

_____

_____

_____

_____

_____

_____

_____

_____

_____

THE FOUNDATION

For any building project, you need a firm foundation, and in order to choose the right foundation, the builder needs to know the size of the structure. In world building terms, the foundation is the mythology, the long history, and/or the recent history of the story world.

For instance:

✗ Flash fiction and short stories only need a minimal foundation, like footers for a shed.

✗ Novellas need a little more foundation, like a grade beam footing for a small house.

✗ Full-length novels need a deep slab foundation.

✗ A series will have a shared deep slab foundation with reinforcing, like an apartment building with many different lives and stories built upon the same architecture. Think of the first floor as the beginning of the mythology, and the top floor as the futuremost time away from the beginning. Think about how the peoples on the floors in between the two perceive their past, their present, and their future. Also, stories from the past become skewed over time and after many re-tellings, and scientific discovery may change the meaning of the stories. For instance, the people on the first floor may have believed a volcano eruption the wrath of an angry god while the people on the tenth floor know the science behind the eruption.

A writer should not place a short story on a deep slab foundation. Nor should a writer build a full-length world structure on footers. In other words, the writer only needs a minimal amount of world building for a short work of fiction, and a full-length novel will fall flat without enough world building. A series requires quite a bit of world building, but not all of it takes place in the first book. It may not all be revealed until the third, or fourth, or eleventh book. Some characters will see aspects of the world that others do not. Remember, the scope of a story world is directly tied to the characters' points of view, not the author's all knowing view from the mountaintop.

Do you expect your story to be a short story, a novella, or a novel? _____

_____

Side Note: A writer never wants to sacrifice story for world building. However, experience does make a difference. If you've already done research on a particular genre such as steampunk or urban fantasy, and have written in those genres, it's easier to write a short story without sacrificing either story or story world.

Creating the Mythology:

Most foundations are made of concrete, which is primarily a mixture of cement and water, with other materials, such as sand or gravel. It is also referred to as liquid stone. This is the perfect description for a story world's foundation.

The concrete of world building is the mixture of elements of the world the writer wants to build, such as a certain magic or science fiction technologies, and the world's inhabitants.

The story world is the cement, and the inhabitants are the water that causes the change.

The inhabitants are fluid. They will have, and will probably go through, several evolutionary changes. Wars, plagues, golden eras, dark ages, all of these will affect the inhabitants and cause change. However, once the bond is made, no matter the changes to the inhabitants or the physical world, the foundation will still be what defines the story world.

Combining the inhabitants with their physical world, their history, and evolution is creating the mythology of the world. It doesn't need to be perfect, and it doesn't need to be detailed to the nth degree. Most of these details are for the writer, not the reader. Bits and pieces will probably be brought out in the story, but not in a year-by-year, or century-by-century, breakdown of events that made the main character what he/she is today.

Things to consider:
- ☒ Are the inhabitants indigenous to the world?
- ☒ Were they conquerors?
- ☒ Were they explorers who got stranded?
- ☒ Were they slaves brought to the world?
- ☒ Were they colonists from another land, planet, or galaxy?

The tone of the story world also takes shape here. Atmosphere and mood are relayed to the reader through the attitudes, thoughts, actions, and dialogue of the characters coupled with the natural setting. Is the tone dark and sinister? Comical? Mysterious? Romantic? Satirical? Gothic? Being conscious of the tone at this stage of the writing will help insure consistency throughout as other elements of the story world are chosen. This is where the story bible can help immensely. It can be used to keep track of the colors, textures, and weather patterns, etc., that set the tone of the scenes and then to use them to paint the story setting.

Many world mythologies contain rituals that pertain to the changing of the seasons, and many of the rituals persisted when the beliefs changed. Whether this type of seasonal ritual exists in the mythology, seasons can bear an important role in the story world. The length of the seasons may help or impede the main character's goal. An abrupt end to a season could be the result of an angry deity, the beginning of an extinction-level event, nuclear fallout, or magical spell.

Developing weather patterns is somewhat complex, with many different variables to consider. I would suggest that unless the story demands unique weather patterns, the writer should stick with the familiar. A desert will be hot and arid, until nightfall when the temperatures drop to dangerously cold. Story worlds that are built close to a planet's equator will be hotter than those built toward the poles. A jungle will have daily periods of rain, snow will be almost non-existence in warmer regions, and plains will flood with too much rain. If there is an abrupt change in the weather patterns, like those listed for seasons, a brief explanation is usually all that is needed.

Time on Earth is measured by intervals. A day equals one complete rotation of the Earth. A year equals one complete rotation of the Earth around the sun. The twenty-four hour day and the division of a year into months is man-made.

Not all societies will have time measurements, nor will they have linear time. Some societies may have the ability to control the flow of time, or travel in time. Some hours of the day may be thought more magical than others, like midnight.

There are many uses for time in speculative fiction. Time may be directly related to the character's destiny if it has been foretold that he is to meet his mortal enemy (and death) on a certain day at a certain time, and no matter how hard he tries not to be there, he cannot seem to escape it. The measurement of time can be an integral part of the story, or as simple as day and night.

What are some elements you want to include in your story world's mythology?

_____

_____

_____

_____

_____

_____

How do these elements affect the main characters? The plot?

_____

_____

_____

_____

_____

_____

What mood or atmosphere do you want your story to have? List some mythology elements that will enhance the mood or atmosphere? _____

_____

_____

_____

Are there any elements, such as weather, time, or real-world mythologies that you need to research? _____

_____

_____

_____

Research/reference materials/websites used: _____

_____

_____

_____

_____

_____

_____

_____

_____

_____

_____

_____

_____

_____

_____

_____

Combining all of the elements, write a detailed mythology for your story world:

_____

_____

_____

_____

_____

_____

_____

_____

_____

_____

_____

_____

_____

_____

_____

_____

_____

_____

_____

_____

_____

_____

The Exterior Walls, Floors, and Roofing

If you've ever shopped for carpet, hardwood, tile, or marble, you know flooring is a major decision and not something just to be walked on. It has to be strong enough and durable enough, to take wear and tear for years. The same holds true for the exterior walls and roofing. The decision to use brick, stone, logs, adobe, or wood for the exterior walls, and slate, tin, or shingles for the roofing, all play into the overall strength of the structure. In building a story world, these elements of the structure are government and military.

Government encompasses everything in the story world. Unfortunately, story world inhabitants can't escape from the government in their everyday lives any more than we can. Like the inhabitants, the government may have gone through, or is going through, or there is the threat of it going through, a major change. However, the writer needs to choose the type of government, the different branches, the laws, the court system, the types of punishments meted out, the types of incarceration, and rehabilitation. This will also determine armies, allies and enemies, the type of spies, and any resistance movements.

Obviously, the more rigid the building material, the more rigid the form of government.

The story world may have one centralized government, or smaller governments each ruling their own part of the story world. It may be directly connected to the story world's religion, or it may develop solely from the need for order.

For flash fiction and short stories, and some novellas, the government may never be a story element, or anything more than a passing reference to the king, or president, etc. In full-length novels and series, it should be structured enough to provide reasoning and balance to the character's actions, non-actions, or point of view. In stories where morality is part of the theme, such as rapid growth of technology, or the banning of magic, the government (and religion) should be developed in detail. You may not need to fill out all of the information asked for in this section. If not, feel free to skip it, except for what's pertinent to your story world.

Writers should research any form of government they intend to use as a model in a story world. I encourage this for two reasons. The first is because if a writer wants to create a story world government from the model of an established governmental system, the writer needs to know exactly how the government is structured. The second is because if a writer wants to break the rules, the writer must first know the rules. (This also applies to all "rules" of writing.) It's also a good idea to do more extensive research on governmental systems to create a unique governmental system for a story world.

Government:

For the purposes of the world building workbook, the government may not need to be fully noted. If, for example, the writer decides on a monarchy system of government, only a few highlights need to be noted because most people know the basic way a monarchy works. However, if the writer decides to combine elements of different governments to create a system unfamiliar to the reader, more extensive notes will be needed.

When creating a totally new system of government, be . . . well, creative. If the story has a governmental system in which computers use logic sequences to decide on laws, how they are interpreted, trade agreements, elections, etc., then why not call it a computocracy? Or comparchy? The labels or titles a writer gives the system and its leaders, while sometimes strange or even comical (depending on the tone of the story), can relay as much information as a few detailed paragraphs on how the system works.

How many government structures are in your story world? _____

What are the core models for each government structure? (simple descriptions are in Appendix B.)

Structure	Who Uses It
☒ Monarchy _____	☒ Socialism _____
☒ Democracy _____	☒ Feudalism _____
☒ Republic _____	☒ Totalitarianism _____
☒ Communism _____	☒ Tribal/Clan _____
☒ Theocracy _____	☒ Anarchy _____
☒ Oligarchy _____	☒ Other _____
☒ Dictatorship _____	

Describe the dominant government, including how leaders are chosen (include advisors, governors, mayors, etc.), the branches of the government and how they operate, checks and balances, how laws are adopted, its philosophy, its diplomatic structure, and its strengths & weaknesses: _____

_____

_____

_____

_____

_____

_____

_____

_____

_____

_____

_____

_____

_____

_____

_____

_____

_____

_____

_____

_____

Describe the other governments, including how leaders are chosen (include advisors, governors, mayors, etc.), the branches of the government and how they operate, checks and balances, how laws are adopted, their philosophies, their diplomatic structure, and their strengths and weaknesses:

2. _____

_____

_____

_____

_____

_____

_____

_____

_____

_____

_____

_____

_____

_____

_____

_____

_____

_____

_____

_____

_____

3. _____

_____

_____

_____

_____

_____

_____

_____

_____

_____

_____

_____

_____

_____

_____

_____

_____

_____

_____

_____

_____

_____

_____

_____

_____

_____

_____

_____

4. _____

_____

_____

_____

_____

_____

_____

_____

_____

_____

_____

_____

_____

_____

_____

_____

_____

_____

_____

_____

_____

_____

_____

_____

_____

_____

5. _____

_____

_____

_____

_____

_____

_____

_____

_____

_____

_____

_____

_____

_____

_____

_____

_____

_____

_____

_____

_____

_____

_____

Which governments are allies and why: _____

_____

_____

_____

_____

_____

Which governments are enemies and why: _____

_____

_____

_____

_____

_____

Describe how food/products/services are traded between governments, including

agreements, money exchanges, and modes of transportation: _____

_____

_____

_____

_____

_____

Describe each government's diplomacy policy (include information about how embassy

locations are chosen, diplomats are chosen, etc): _____

_____

_____

_____

_____

_____

Describe any secret government classes such as spies, secret police, etc. for each government (including why they are needed and how recruits are chosen): _____

_____

_____

_____

_____

_____

_____

_____

_____

_____

_____

Describe what domestic powers each governments holds (e.g. births, deaths, marriages, divorces, religion, educations, etc.) and the justifications for these powers:

_____

_____

_____

_____

_____

_____

_____

_____

_____

_____

_____

Describe the judicial system for each government from the lowest court to the highest court (including any specialized courts): _____

_____

_____

_____

_____

_____

_____

_____

_____

_____

_____

_____

_____

Are there any vigilante/resistance groups opposing any of the story world's governments? If so, describe their agendas, their ranks, how they recruit, how they spread propaganda, etc.:

_____

_____

_____

_____

_____

_____

_____

Describe the police system for each government (from local, to regional, to national, to world): _____

_____

_____

_____

_____

_____

_____

_____

_____

_____

_____

_____

_____

_____

Describe the prison system, including how they are built, what types of prisons there are (buildings, walled cities, penal colonies on other continents, moons, etc.) intake procedures, whether they are privately or government owned, internal punishments/rewards, prison labor (e.g. chain gangs), how sentences are served, who determines parole/release, etc.

_____

_____

_____

_____

_____

_____

Research/reference materials/websites used:

_____

_____

_____

_____

_____

_____

_____

_____

_____

_____

_____

_____

_____

_____

_____

_____

_____

_____

_____

_____

_____

_____

_____

_____

_____

Military:

Walls and roof also protect the inhabitants of the structure from the elements, exposure, and attackers, and provide a sense of security. This represents the military.

Some sort of military force is needed in every type of society. Otherwise, the society faces the possibility of being invaded and overtaken, or annihilated by an aggressive society. The landscape of the story world and the type of government usually determines the type of military.

If the military is to play an integral role in a story, then special attention should be paid to the military, as it is usually a society unto itself. The hierarchy, or chain of command, should be established with a leader or leaders, officers, non-commissioned officers, and the rank and file.

Members may be drafted or conscripted, they may volunteer, or perhaps during wartime, prisoners are placed in the front lines with promises of freedom if they survive. There may be a special segment of the citizenry from which all soldiers or warriors are bred. Whatever the case, there will probably be some sort of induction ceremony, and another ceremony when a certain rank is achieved if moving up in rank is allowed. There will be some sort of recognition and decorations for honor, or bravery, or mastering a certain skill. There will be privileges that come with certain ranks.

A military will also have its own set of rules and regulations and a set of punishments for those who break them. The military court system will have its own rules, with military advocates and judges. In wartime, it may be no more than a kangaroo court, or mock trial, with no advocacy for the accused and with the outcome determined beforehand.

Just as a government must be funded, a military must also be compensated. There are many and various methods for a government to generate income, whether it be by taxes, tribute, or tithes. A portion of that income must be provided to the military forces. We've all heard the old saying that an army travels on its stomach. A hungry army will become a pack of marauders. An unpaid army will become mercenaries. The government will be faced with the task of providing food, weapons, uniforms, transportation, training, etc., for the warriors or soldiers, and money for expenses has to be generated through income.

If martial law is not in effect, then some other type of police force is necessary. It will also have a chain of command, specialized education, honors, and decorations like the military. Most often, a police force is governed locally and under the same laws as the citizenry. Police, as well as the criminals, will answer in a court of law. The way the court system functions will be determined by the type of government the writer has chosen.

This does not mean, however, that the local police force will always adhere to a certain code of conduct. Power corrupts, and widespread corruption may turn a local police force into something akin to a brute squad that terrorizes the citizens and uses a macabre caricature of the laws, along with their weapons, to enforce their power over the population.

The government may also have secret police, which quite naturally do not stay secret for very long. It is more a fear of the _idea_ of your (or your family) being taken from your home (beaten, drugged, or unconscious) to some underground facility by the secret police, than the act itself that keeps the average citizen from speaking out against the government.

Spy networks are the red headed step-children of the government. They belong to the government, but no governmental official wants to acknowledge their existence. Spies can be used to gather information and intelligence on another government, another army, or its own country's citizenry. If the government is based on technology or corporate entities, one branch may use spies to ensure the balance of power within the government, especially if there is tension between the different government branches.

This is another place vigilante groups appear. If there is no formal system of law, or in a city, town, or village that is so distant from the center of law and government it can't be policed by normal means, vigilante groups pop up. Unfortunately, it is often a case of good intentions turned bad. Citizens may start out with a vigilance committee, people who take it upon themselves to keep a watchful eye out for those in their community who break the rules or try to take undue advantage of situations. The vigilante group, left unchecked, will become tyrannical, and any slight or offense, according to the group's edicts, is dealt with harshly.

A vigilante group may also come to being by a few people who don't like the way the current law official handles a certain type of crime. These people don't need further proof, or a court of law to tell them a person is guilty, and by sheer force, they will exact punishment. Vigilante groups were common in the American west during the pioneer days and were motivated by greed and power. Unfortunately they also appeared in the South, which was motivated by prejudice. Vigilante groups can also be motivated by religion, or something more visceral, like starvation or lack of medical attention.

For each military, describe the different uniforms, hierarchy, the different branches, how the military is compensated/housed/feed/clothed, how advancement within the ranks is achieved, military rewards/punishments, penalty for desertion, any laws that only relate to military personnel, and any weapons, magics, or technologies only available to the military:

Dominant Military: _____

_____

_____

_____

_____

_____

_____

_____

_____

_____

_____

_____

_____

_____

_____

_____

_____

_____

_____

_____

_____

_____

_____

_____

2.

3._____

_____

_____

_____

_____

_____

_____

_____

_____

_____

_____

_____

_____

_____

_____

_____

_____

_____

_____

_____

_____

_____

_____

_____

_____

_____

_____

_____

_____

4.

5. _____

_____

_____

_____

_____

_____

_____

_____

_____

_____

_____

_____

_____

_____

_____

_____

_____

_____

_____

_____

_____

_____

_____

Research/reference materials/websites used:

_____

_____

_____

_____

_____

_____

_____

_____

_____

_____

_____

_____

_____

_____

_____

_____

_____

_____

_____

_____

_____

_____

_____

The Electrical, Plumbing, and Heating & Air

Electrical lines, plumbing lines, and venting systems form a complex web throughout a building under the floors and in walls and ceilings. These conduits provide energy, water, cool air in the summer and warm air in the winter. They represent economy and education. And due to the fact that they are so interwoven with the floors, walls, and ceiling, they are most often a result of the type of government and/or societies created, or they are the basis of the government and/or societies.

However, just as the electrical lines are not one-size-fits-all, neither should the story world's education be accessible to, or wanted by, every inhabitant. Not all closets have lights, and you can't plug your toaster into a 220-volt receptacle. Some rooms will be illuminated with blinding overhead lights, while others may only have crude oil lamps. There are, of course, exceptions. The most common is a theocracy. The beliefs are forced upon the population, usually with violent or deadly consequences for those who refuse to accept the one and only recognized religion. However, in spite of the consequences, there are oftentimes dissenters.

Economy

The story world's economy will also stem from the system of government. Will the government use taxation to raise the money required to run, or will it own all businesses, farms, manufacturing, etc., and provide for its citizens? Will it be a combination of economies, or one that provides for the elite from the taxation of the average citizen or vice-versa?

It is important to make logical choices concerning economies as they relate to the government. It is highly unlikely that a democracy will have a spoils of war economic system. Any writer who creates a government should take as much care to create an economic system that complements the government. Does this mean a government and economic system that are incongruent cannot work in a story world? No, it doesn't. However, it takes great care and skill to make them believable.

What type of economic system(s) does the world have? (Simple descriptions of several economic systems are described in Appendix C.)

- ☒ Capitalist
- ☒ Free Market
- ☒ Planned
- ☒ Spoils of War
- ☒ Other (describe) _____

_____

_____

- ☒ Tribute
- ☒ Barter
- ☒ Corporate Owned
- ☒ None

Describe the dominant economic system, including the types of currency used, exchange rates, the banking structure, government or other oversight, counterfeiting techniques, protocols for economic collapse, etc. _____

_____

_____

_____

_____

_____

_____

_____

_____

_____

_____

_____

_____

_____

2: _____

_____

_____

_____

_____

_____

_____

_____

_____

_____

_____

_____

_____

_____

_____

_____

_____

_____

_____

_____

_____

_____

_____

_____

3: _____

_____

_____

_____

_____

_____

_____

_____

_____

_____

_____

_____

_____

_____

_____

_____

_____

_____

_____

_____

_____

_____

_____

_____

_____

4: _____

_____

_____

_____

_____

_____

_____

_____

_____

_____

_____

_____

_____

_____

_____

_____

_____

_____

_____

_____

_____

_____

_____

_____

5: _____

_____

_____

_____

_____

_____

_____

_____

_____

_____

_____

_____

_____

_____

_____

_____

_____

_____

_____

_____

_____

_____

_____

_____

_____

_____

_____

_____

_____

Research/reference materials/websites used:

_____

_____

_____

_____

_____

_____

_____

_____

_____

_____

_____

_____

_____

_____

_____

_____

_____

_____

_____

_____

_____

_____

_____

_____

Education

With a government in place, and an economic system in place, the next major part of the story world that affects the characters is the educational system.

The character only knows what he is taught. As with point of view, the characters do not share in the omniscience of the writer. Learning, growing, and changing are all part of the character's journey through the story.

The type of government and economic system usually determines the kind of education a character receives. An egalitarian government may provide the same education to every child. A free market economic system may only provide the level of education commensurate with the family income. A theocracy will provide an education based on the religious beliefs and will not introduce theories, magics, or other curricula that are in contrast to those religious beliefs.

Social position within a society may determine the educational opportunities. Those of a higher status, such as a peer of the realm, will receive a better education than the peasants. A prince will probably learn a great deal in science, mathematics, diplomacy, warfare, justice, and hunting, but may not know how to field dress an animal for eating, or how to grow crops.

A character who has had a proper academic education may not understand the need for games. A character who expects to spend his life as a laborer may not want to learn to read.

A leader who wants to enslave a society, or a specific sector of a society, will probably outlaw any type of education. A conquering society may do the same. Restricting or denying education takes away a major component of freedom from those being suppressed or enslaved.

For specialized characters, such as vampires, some abilities may exist at birth, but the character will need to learn how to use the ability. He may have a knack for dematerializing with almost no instruction, but fails at completely removing a human's memory even after years of trying.

Also, for specialized characters who have magical or psychic abilities, they may be able to acquire knowledge by reading someone's mind or connecting with an object. Not all knowledge is learned through study and education.

What type of educational system does the story world have?

- ☒ Free to All
- ☒ Government controlled
- ☒ Religion controlled
- ☒ Only to the rich
- ☒ Only to royalty
- ☒ Only to religious leaders
- ☒ Private institution only
- ☒ Specialized (testing for math, science, etc., to determine education)
- ☒ Through apprenticeship, indentured servitude, etc.
- ☒ Other (describe) _____

Describe how the dominant education system works, such as the age education starts, how long it lasts, courses of study, graduation ceremonies, higher education, qualifications for teaching, etc. _____

_____

_____

_____

_____

_____

_____

_____

_____

_____

_____

_____

_____

2: _____

3: _____

4: _____

_____

_____

_____

_____

_____

_____

_____

_____

_____

_____

_____

_____

_____

_____

_____

_____

_____

_____

_____

_____

_____

_____

_____

5: _____

List and describe any specialized fields of study relating to the magics or technologies in your story world: _____

_____

_____

_____

_____

_____

_____

_____

_____

_____

_____

_____

_____

_____

_____

_____

_____

_____

_____

_____

_____

_____

_____

Research/reference materials/websites used:

_____

_____

_____

_____

_____

_____

_____

_____

_____

_____

_____

_____

_____

_____

_____

_____

_____

_____

_____

_____

_____

_____

_____

_____

_____

The Ceiling

The ceiling is an interesting piece of architecture. It is aesthetically pleasing, as its patterned plaster (or tiles) hide the ugly maze of pipes, wires, and vents from our view. It also provides a bit of protection by filtering some sounds, and keeping inhabitants dry when there is a leak in the roof. The ceiling represents religion, or a belief system, whether or not it has a supernatural deity.

Religions can originate from a number of different scenarios. There are primitive religions and belief systems, such as sun worshippers, where religion started as a way to explain supernatural or scientific concepts primitive cultures could not understand. Organized religions are based on the teachings of a spiritual being. Cults can idolize anything in the universe, and other belief systems can be based on magic, science, or nature.

The one thing a religion or belief system needs is people who believe with enough force or influence to propagate the belief. This can be accomplished by either the performance of a miracle, or the charismatic ability of a prophet, disciple, priest, or mystic to persuade others to join them in worship.

In the case of a cult or some other insular group, the actual membership may be small and remain segregated outside of normal society. Depending on the belief system of the cult, their "holy land" could be a commune or a compound.

However, whether it be a state religion, free religion, cult, sun worshipper, etc., rituals will play a large part in the experience. The rituals may include fire or water for cleansing and purification, blood for sacrifice, wine or hallucinogenic drugs to free the spirit from the body or to allow those participating to hear the words of a prophecy.

This is also the part of the story world where taboos, superstitions, and traditions will develop, either from fear of a religious figure, fear of the government, or lack of education.

Superstitions will also probably long outlive their believability. It is believed that knocking on wood dates back to ancient times when people thought good spirits lived in trees.

Some superstitions have subtle changes from region to region. What happens if your palm itches? If my left palm itches, nothing happens, but if my right palm itches, I can expect money to come my way. Others will tell you if their left palm itches, they expect to lose money. Even within a small group of people, a few of them will have a different interpretation of itchy palms.

Then there are colloquial superstitions that haven't traveled far from their origins. I've always heard that if you count the number of train cars while stopped at the track, that will be the number of days until someone in your family dies. Yet, I have seldom heard of this superstition outside of my community.

The same concepts hold true for taboos and traditions. A world or society with religious influences will probably have superstitions and taboos dealing with demons and devils. A world or society that lacks education may have a monthly ceremony with offerings of their finest crops to the sky so the good rain will continue to come. A world or society based on technology may consider it taboo to own a pencil.

There may also be taboos concerning sex. No signs of affection, like holding hands or kissing, in public. Perhaps sex is only allowed on certain days of the month, or when a couple is trying to have a baby. Rape could be a heinous crime, or it could be seen as a man's right. Oral sex, or other types, may be outlawed. Or taboos can travel into the outrageous. It might be against the law or religion for someone with blonde hair to marry or have sex with someone with red hair or green eyes. Or maybe only two people who are the same height can have sex.

This is definitely a subject the writer can have fun with, especially if building a world where a warrior society plays a major role in the story. To breed the strongest and best fighters of the species, rules and taboos regarding sex will have an impact. They will also have an impact on any society in which certain traits, such as intellect, artistic ability, strength, or looks are revered over others.

Many superstitions and taboos have remedies that will negate the consequences. Spill some salt? Throw a pinch over your left shoulder. Break a mirror? Bury it under the moonlight. So, in dealing with superstitions and taboos, writers should think not only of the origins and consequences but also of the out clauses.

Traditions can appear in many ways. Wedding and funeral traditions are probably the most common, but traditions can be woven into a story at almost any event. The birth of a child, the gathering of crops, buying or building a house, receiving a new weapon, and completing a level of education can be associated with some type of tradition.

Holidays are also traditions--a time set aside, whether it be a day, a week, or longer, for feasts, recreation, remembrance, etc. Perhaps weddings can only occur on a certain holiday. A serious and staid society may have a holiday when atavistic behavior emerges, either by choice or because it is brought about by some genetic anomaly or supernatural force.

Religion

Does religion play a vital or pivotal role in the story? _____

Is it based on a real-world religion? If yes, which one? Briefly describe it: _____

_____

_____

Is the dominant a universal religion, a world religion, a state religion, or is there religious

freedom? _____

_____

If it's a universal religion, how is it enforced/sustained? _____

_____

_____

If any other religions play a role in the story, are they world religions, state religions, or local

religions? Are they an offshoot of the dominant religion? Are there any cults?_____

_____

_____

_____

Describe the dominant religion including the origins, beliefs, sacraments, icons, rites, rituals,

indoctrination, special foods/garments/abilities, the hierarchy of the religious leaders, art,

hymns, special ceremonies/services, writings, celebrations, tithing, how it deals with other

religions and atheists, etc.:_____

_____

_____

_____

_____

_____

_____

2: _____

_____

_____

_____

_____

_____

_____

_____

_____

_____

_____

_____

_____

_____

_____

_____

_____

_____

_____

_____

_____

_____

_____

3: _____

4: _____

_____

_____

_____

_____

_____

_____

_____

_____

_____

_____

_____

_____

_____

_____

_____

_____

_____

_____

_____

_____

_____

_____

_____

_____

_____

_____

5: _____

Other small sect religions: _____

_____

_____

_____

_____

_____

_____

_____

_____

_____

_____

Describe any cults: _____

_____

_____

_____

_____

_____

_____

_____

_____

_____

_____

_____

_____

_____

Research/reference materials/websites used:

Superstitions & their origins: _____

_____

_____

_____

_____

_____

_____

_____

Taboos & their origins: _____

_____

_____

_____

_____

_____

_____

_____

_____

Traditions & their origins: _____

_____

_____

_____

_____

_____

_____

_____

Research/reference materials/websites used:

Doors and Windows

In the story world structure, doors and windows represent technologies, magic, and culture. Windows allow illumination, in the form of science, ideas and imagination, to enter the structure. Doors allow guests to enter and exit, and those guests may bring new ideas, new technologies, new arts and culture into the structure. Doors and windows are also risky, as it is through those same elements a burglar may enter and steal ideas and technologies. Or, someone disguised as a guest may actually have malicious intent.

A guest may also innocently introduce some idea, form of art, or technology to the inhabitants that the government or religious leaders are trying to keep out. A dark age period occurs when all the doors are kept shut and the windows are kept covered. A golden age occurs when the doors and windows are kept open and a great flow of technological or other type of advancement takes place.

Technology, magic, and culture develop over a long period of time, and like education and religion may only be available to the government or a select class within society. For example, government farms may have state of the art machinery, while the ordinary citizen is only allowed a horse-drawn plow.

If the writer decides on a peaceful, utopian world in which the inhabitants are centered solely on culture and philosophy, there is the risk of the world being easily conquered. If a world is based on magic, there is the risk of losing magical ability to technology. If a world is technology based, there is the risk of it destroying itself. No one method is perfect, and magic may lead to technology, or technology may lead to more leisure time to pursue art and culture. Or, there may be a mixture.

TECHNOLOGY

Technology is fluid and changes with the needs, discoveries, and natural resources of the story world. Very few technologies are discovered through a "eureka" moment or by accident. There is a logical path to founding technologies. Clothing for the story world probably started with animal skins, then to a cloth once the inhabitants discovered a way to sheer the sheep, spin thread, and then weave it into cloth. However, it was probably rough against the skin, tore easily, and didn't last very long. So, a better loom was built for a stronger, better weave, then dyes were added for different colors. From there, more raw materials provide different types of materials, some better, prettier, or more expensive to weave than others. Patterns and fashions emerged from the prettier, more expensive cloths, and in a matter of a hundred years or so, the poorer classes are fated to wear the lower quality materials while the richer classes wear silk. Once demand for more clothes, and even better quality comes about, machines are developed.

The things to remember regarding technologies are the basic needs of the inhabitants. Food, clothing, shelter, medicine, defense, and the availability of raw materials (animals, vegetables, fruits, wood, herbs, copper, iron, etc.) to fill those needs will determine the types of technologies that will logically come about as the civilization grows. Resist the temptation to have technologies in the story world that appear illogical or ahead of their time. Lost technologies might be found as a quest element of the story, but the inhabitants won't understand them or know how to use them.

Describe the dominant technologies, including how they were discovered, how they're manufactured, how they're disposed of after final use, what they're used for, any restrictions of use, side effects (like nuclear waste), who controls manufacturing and use, etc.:

_____

_____

_____

_____

_____

_____

_____

_____

_____

_____

_____

_____

_____

_____

_____

_____

_____

_____

_____

_____

_____

_____

Research/reference materials/websites used:

Magic

Magic may be inborn or taught, but even if the magic is inborn, the skill must be developed. Children must be taught the laws of the magic they control. Are any types of magic outlawed or forbidden? Are all individuals taught to perform the same levels of magic? Is there something genetically, environmentally, or magically that controls how far an individual may advance in his skill? Is magic skill connected only to the strength of the mind, or to the strength of body as well? Does the magic evolve with the needs of the world? Can new magic be developed? Can magic be taken away, stripped, or restrained as punishment?

An important note to remember about magic. It isn't completely devoid of technology. Before the flying carpet is loaded up and taken on vacation, we look again at the cloth example. The knowledge of how to sheer wool from a sheep and produce thread from the wool must be understood, as well as how to dye the thread and then weave it into cloth. The method of manufacturing must be known before it can be duplicated in magic. Many times, magic and technology will develop concurrently and diverge when a society decides one is more important than the other.

There are, of course, exceptions. The ability to fly, or to become invisible, might be inborn magic. In writing a world where magic is predominant, it behooves the writer to decide which magic skills and abilities are natural to the inhabitants and which are learned.

Describe the magic systems, including how they originated, their rules, who's allowed to use them, the hierarchy of the practitioners, whether its inborn or taught, how it's used, any restrictions of use, side effects (like broken psyches), any laws/regulations that cover magic use, any special objects used, any special ceremonies/rites/rituals/clothing, etc.:

_____

_____

_____

_____

_____

_____

_____

_____

_____

_____

_____

_____

_____

_____

_____

_____

_____

_____

_____

_____

_____

Research/reference materials/websites used:

The Healing Arts

It's easy to forget the healing arts—until a character in the story requires medical attention. Sometimes an author gets lucky and a physician, witch doctor, or shaman is the obvious choice of healer for the story line. And sometimes it is not clear how an injured character can be healed. If the character has traveled from his homeland where the medical arts are directly related to the technology, would the character look for a doctor? Probably, but what the character finds is perhaps closer to the witch doctor or some other sort of magical healing the character will not want to trust.

Specialized characters will require specialized healing arts. A vampire, werewolf, or alien who is injured cannot be taken to a conventional hospital. Not only will their injuries appear strange to contemporary doctors, but the doctors will have no way to determine a treatment. Perhaps antibiotics are poisonous or snake venom is a pain killer. A little forethought to the healing arts can prevent an author from having to make a sudden stop in the story in order to work it out.

Describe the healing arts, including the education/magic required, if there are any faith healers, if it's controlled by the government or the private sector, if medical care is available to everyone or if it's restricted, if there's an insurance system, if there are any protocols in place for plagues, viral outbreaks, germ warfare, etc. :

_____

_____

_____

_____

_____

_____

_____

_____

_____

_____

_____

_____

_____

_____

_____

_____

_____

_____

_____

_____

_____

Research/reference materials/websites used:

Culture

Culture will grow out of a combination of religion, technology, and/or magic. Pretty and handsome are culturally developed concepts, as are art, music, and even eating habits. Myths, legends, and fairytales are cultural elements. The appropriate way for men and women to wear their hair, to dress, to speak, and to act in each other's presence are cultural elements. Proper etiquette, in public and in private, will all be born of the story world's culture. Is eating in public a taboo? What about showing your teeth, your ears, your knees? Is whistling considered to be an invitation to fight? If you kiss someone of the opposite sex on the cheek, is it a sign of engagement?

When developing story world culture, does it need to be diverse or stringent? Will the emperor or religious leader always decide what is culturally acceptable, or will culture and customs develop solely from the inhabitants? Are there different cultural standards for the different classes of society? What are the punishments for ignoring the cultural restrictions? Banishment, penance, community service, jail, death?

Describe the story world's culture, including manners (public & private), customs, the diversity of different races, how food is flavored & cooked, how people are treated if they are addicted to alcohol, drugs, gambling, sex, etc, how women are treated, how children are treated, how men are treated, how pets are treated, how wildlife is treated (natural resources, zoos), how people say hello, goodbye, socially acceptable behavior, etc.:

_____

_____

_____

_____

_____

_____

_____

_____

_____

_____

_____

_____

_____

_____

_____

_____

_____

_____

_____

_____

_____

Research/reference materials/websites used:

_____

_____

_____

_____

_____

_____

_____

_____

_____

_____

_____

_____

_____

_____

_____

_____

_____

_____

_____

_____

_____

_____

_____

Infrastructure

This is also where the story world's infrastructure will take shape. Technology, aesthetics, and raw materials will determine the roadways, the shape and height of buildings, the traffic system, the types of energy available for items like vehicles and other forms of transportation (land, water, and air), appliances, and communications.

In addition, recreation and types of entertainment--concerts, plays, movies, television, exhibits, sporting events, paintings, books, etc., will begin here and evolve as the story world's societies evolve.

Describe the story world's infrastructure:

_____

_____

_____

_____

_____

_____

_____

_____

_____

_____

_____

_____

_____

_____

_____

_____

_____

_____

_____

_____

_____

_____

Research/reference materials/websites used:

Social Classes and Societies

Just as the interior walls of a structure form different types of rooms, the interior walls of the story structure form different types of social classes and societies. The elite will be separated from the poor. The armies will be separated from the general population. The rich and famous will have a different societal circle than the laborer. Political figures will also have their own social class.

Plan the social classes carefully. As an example, a house needs a number of rooms to be comfortably functional: a kitchen, living room (or great room), bedrooms, bathrooms, closets, laundry, etc., all proportionate to the inhabitants' needs. Equate social classes with the function, but not necessarily the size, of the corresponding rooms. The elite may equate to an opulent master bedroom. The famous may equate with the great room, where they can be seen and admired by all. The white-collar society may have a den or modest bedroom. The laborers may equate to the kitchen or laundry. If the world has slaves or serfs, they may equate to the closets, or garages.

Hallways are the connectors. The social classes must interact with each other, and societies from different worlds must interact with each other. The farmer must get his food to the market or grocer, who in turn sells it to the cook. The hallways may be short or long, wide or narrow, depending on how much interaction the writer needs between the social classes and societies. Some hallways may even be blocked.

These corridors will also determine commerce. Is gold or some other precious stone or metal the legal tender of the different societies? Or, does one society use gold while another society uses the barter system? Do the societies trade goods and services with each other? How do they determine the trade value from one system of commerce to another?

As a civilization develops, so will its social classes. Unfortunately, some sectors of society will always be poor while others are rich. Some are fated to be workers while others are fated to be thinkers, artists, priests, or leaders.

How these different social classes interact with each other is the element that brings life to the story. Despite the fact that the societies may disdain each other, they will be inter-dependent and rely on members of their own society as well as others to retain the level of social status they have acquired.

Money may decide the difference in the societies, or intelligence levels, or artistic ability, or fighting ability. Tailor the classes within the societies to the story world and don't throw in a class or society just to make a social statement. For instance, in a utopian society, the classes may go from good to best, without a poor class of people, while in a dystopian society, they may go from apathy to worst without a moral class of people. This doesn't mean an individual won't be poor or moral within those societies, only that there won't be a large segment of the population that fits the definition of poor or moral. Also, jealousies, prejudices, and other types of hate based on differences, or some perceived wrong, or perceived inferiority/superiority will emerge.

Each society in the story world will have its own social classes. The elite may not interact with the working class, unless or until some story element forces them to work together. However, it is almost impossible to truly segregate the classes. After all, it is the working class family who will pay to see the famous actor on stage, thus insuring the actor will remain elite. The rich will most likely have servants or slaves. Scientists will have assistants, or possibly sentient specimens. Starship pilots will have a crew.

A common story element is the ability of a character to rise above the social station to which he was born, so plan social classes and their interactions carefully.

The protagonist may or may not fit into the social class of his birth. It makes for great conflict when a peacemaker is born into a warrior class or a scientist is born into a religious class.

And just as each society will have its own social classes, each world will have its own societies and classes.

Building only one society in a story world has the advantage of not having to maintain a lot of details, but most story worlds will require at least two vastly different societies. In order to make them interact, the writer must build corridors, or portals, through which they interact.

This means first and foremost, the societies must find a way to communicate. This may come as a shock, but not all foreign/alien societies speak English with a British accent. Therefore, the writer needs a path of communication before anything else. This doesn't mean the writer must create a language and add it to the written page, but some reference must be made to different dialects, languages, etc. Or, the universal translator device, mechanical or magical, should be close by.

A note about languages. One to ten words and/or phrases from a made-up language within the prose is acceptable if the meaning of the words can be discerned from the text. However, writing whole paragraphs or even a few sentences in a made-up language can be irritating to the reader. If a 50-page glossary is needed to give definitions for the language used in the story, it is probably too much. As writers, we love words and like to make up the languages our characters speak. However, for any writer who feels it necessary to compile an entire language, I suggest that it be a special project for the author's website, or a companion book for a series, other than trying to wow the reader with linguistic skills.

Once communication has been established, trading routes can be negotiated, arranged marriages can take place, and competitions can be arranged, athletic, artistic, or scientific. Diplomats will need to be trained and embassies built.

Some of the different societies' traditions, beliefs, taboos, and histories can be similar, but some will clash. Will the differences be enough to spark a feud? A war? Will two or more societies overlook their differences to unite against a common threat, be it an enemy society, a hoard of dragons, a plague?

Describe the story world's classes — keeping in mind that the most important motivation for any class is food, clothing, shelter & security, include the societies and classes for specialized segments of the population such as weres, fairies, supernatural creatures, demons, angels, sorcerers, witches, dwarves, giants, etc, classes for servants & slaves, artists, religious sects (such as a commune) & cults, societal norms for the upper, middle & lower classes and how they interact, etc. :

_____

_____

_____

_____

_____

_____

_____

_____

_____

_____

_____

_____

_____

_____

_____

_____

_____

_____

_____

_____

_____

Research/reference materials/websites used:

_____

_____

_____

_____

_____

_____

_____

_____

_____

_____

_____

_____

_____

_____

_____

_____

_____

_____

_____

_____

_____

_____

_____

GEOGRAPHY

Humans and humanoids require water to live, so most early colonists and pioneers settled near large bodies of water. However, if the character is rock-like and requires lava, an active volcano would be the prime real estate. When considering the geography of a story world, it is wise to plan a little bit. Serendipity is suspect in fiction. An accidental discovery of a needed resource provokes doubt. If purple water is needed in the magic potion during the climax, its discovery should be noted and then dismissed somewhere in the beginning of the story. This is similar in concept to Chekhov's Gun — if there's a gun on the mantle in Act I, it must go off in Act II.

Some writers use maps, while others depend solely on the cinematic view in their mind's eye.

For novels in which the story (or parts of the story) takes place in a historical period, such as Regency England, maps can usually be found.

Or, the basic outlines of ancient maps can be used for boundaries of the fictional world. Archipelagos can be added to existing maps (whether contemporary or ancient), boundaries can be moved, mountains and rivers can be added or deleted. And don't forget more interesting geographical features. Volcanoes, geysers, underground lakes and waterfalls, an oasis, salt lakes, tar pits, craters, and quicksand are some uncommon elements a writer might incorporate into the geography of the story world.

A Special Note About Geography

Not discounting the fantastic writers who have managed to write fantastic stories with a one-climate planet as the setting, a planet with only one climate, such as a water planet, or an ice planet, or a desert planet, is extremely implausible if you're writing hard science fiction. While it may make for great visual effects in movies, the effect in literature is less than stunning. A civilization would need to be small, a settlement or colony perhaps, in order to survive on such a planet as the raw materials needed to maintain a civilization would be scarce. Settlers with terraforming capabilities might be able to colonize a small parcel of land and thrive on such a planet, but a large population of say, boat dwellers, is unlikely. Where did they get the materials to build boats? And how did they manage evolutionary change without drowning or adapting to the water? Exactly; they wouldn't have. They would have evolved to a species that lives in the sea.

With the inherent problems of creating a believable evolution for humanoid characters on a one-climate planet, it is advisable for the writer not to attempt it.

One exception, and isn't there always an exception, is a natural disaster or an angry deity that causes a once lush multi-climate planet to become a one-climate planet. Still, the inherent difficulties of preparedness of the inhabitants, if they have time to prepare, and the coping mechanisms needed for survival in such a new environment are difficult hurdles for the writer to overcome. The basics--food, water, shelter, clothing, and medical issues--must all be addressed. From there, the need for order or fear of future retribution by the deity will bring about a system of government, etc. The world building in this case all happens on the written page.

For those writers who are visual, or for any writer who just needs a little visual stimulation to help with the landscaping, there are some great websites. Google's Sketch Up (www.sketchup.com) has tools for drawing a city block, a district, or a whole city in 3D. A search for fantasy art can provide some great inspiration, as well as searches for pictures of jungles, the Antarctica, deserts, ghost towns, strange architecture, and outer space.

Describe all of your story worlds settings: _____

_____

Research/reference materials/websites used:

_____

_____

_____

_____

_____

_____

_____

_____

_____

_____

_____

_____

_____

_____

_____

_____

_____

_____

_____

_____

_____

_____

_____

_____

Decorations

Once the structure is complete, it's time to add the finishing touches--the furniture, the wall hangings, the knick-knacks, all of the decorative pieces added to a home. This is the point at which the writer decides on clothing, jewelry, status symbols for the social classes and societies, hairstyles, plants, pets, food, drink, toys, games, etc.

These are the specific descriptions that will connect the reader to the story. The universalisms. The homey touches each of the readers will use to identify with the story world and the characters.

A bed is a bed in any setting. It may be soft or made of stone, but it is still a place to sleep. The same holds true for other furniture, as well as things like forks, stoves, lamps, clothing, and transportation. All of these items have the same basic function, no matter the society or world in which they are used. Use vivid descriptions of these types of everyday items to connect the reader to the story world the same way vivid descriptions are used in bringing the fantastic elements of the story world to life.

Writing detailed description is hard. The words should paint a recognizable picture in the readers' minds without boring them to tears. And it should be done on the sly. It isn't wise to have characters remark on everyday objects just to bring them to the readers' attention. Don't write about the strange shape or style of a coffee mug, have one character throw it at another character, or into a fireplace. An exotic, intricate hairdo is boring, unless it's falling apart in a love scene, or floating in icy cold water in a death scene. In other words, make the details active and part of the story.

Describe your story worlds decorations:

_____

_____

_____

_____

_____

_____

_____

_____

_____

_____

_____

_____

_____

_____

_____

_____

_____

_____

_____

_____

_____

_____

_____

_____

_____

Research/reference materials/websites used:

_____

_____

_____

_____

_____

_____

_____

_____

_____

_____

_____

_____

_____

_____

_____

_____

_____

_____

_____

_____

_____

_____

_____

The Finished Product

Combining the story world with the characters and plot takes a little practice. The beginning writer may be tempted to write pages and pages of story world history and description to explain the actions of the characters. This sort of information dump doesn't advance the story. As I mentioned at the beginning, elements of the story world need to be woven like the threads of a tapestry.

Ease readers into the story world in such a way that they don't realize they've crossed the threshold from realty to fantasy. Leave a trail of breadcrumbs for them to follow and provide the pertinent story world elements through action and dialogue.

Don't rely on a well-crafted story world to carry a thin plot, or a well-crafted plot to stand on a skeletal story world. It takes both to create a story readers will remember.

Scene Management

The devil is in the details. Keeping track of a character's eye color, hair color, and sometimes their name, in any piece of fiction is a daunting task. Even the bestsellers sometimes change a character's detail in the middle of the book. In a speculative fiction work, the number of details is doubled or tripled, and harder to remember.

I am not a plotter by nature, and for me most plotting tools sound great in theory, but I struggle with the application. However, scene management, as it pertains to world building, is a tool that incorporates a little bit of plotting with story world mapping.

For scene management, use poster board, notebook paper, numbered note cards, a wiki, or whatever works with your writing style. Blocks drawn on the poster board or paper represent the different scenes in the novel. If using note cards, the numbers will correlate to the scenes. If using a wiki, each page will correlate to a scene. The method is similar to story boarding, except for the information.

With this method, the first step is the setting; ancient Egypt, a space craft, a laboratory, etc.

The second step is the visceral information. Add details like dark or light, hot or cold, snow, rain or sunshine, engine sounds, the scent of sanitizers, the grit of sand in the character's eyes or boots, anything that breathes life into the setting.

The third step is to add the details like the purple water needed for the potion, and the other clutter found in the scene environment and the mood or tone. A carnival, with its dancing lights, loud music, fast rides, games of chance, and strange characters might be great fun for one character while another character might find the same scene creepy or sinister.

The fourth step is to add the action. Does the character start in scene, enter the scene, or exit the scene? Does the character leave an object, take an object, or simply observe? Items such as clothing, sunglasses, weapons, purses, wallets, backpacks, etc., move through the setting with the character. Use the map to make sure the knife in the character's hand at the beginning of the scene doesn't magically move to a sheath in the character's boot at the end of the scene. Or that a piece of clothing torn in a fight doesn't magically repair itself in the next scene.

The fifth, and final, step is to add the directing signs. They can either be for the writer's reference, or for mapping the characters' movements. For the writer's reference, it could be a quick note that the character needs to go through the howling forest before he crosses the river. For mapping the characters' movements, it could be that the character found the purple water, but dismissed it. Instinctively, the reader will know it has some importance, but the need for purple water isn't immediate. Perhaps the immediate need of the character was a clue to the location of a magic sword. The directing signs should lead the reader to the next logical setting, either to find another clue or to find the sword. It may not be the next scene, but even if it is three or four scenes later, the reader will have no problem keeping up because of the directing signs.

Steps can be added as they are needed. Perhaps a character in the story is morphing, or showing symptoms of a disease. Perhaps the oceans are evaporating, or the ice caps are melting. A writer can make sure of a logical progression of these events using scene management.

Does all this scene management stuff sound a little like plotting? It is, in a way. Although it doesn't have the growth of the characters, or the events of each scene, it does give the writer some idea of where the story is going. It is also proof that story and story world are intertwined, and that everything in the story relates to the story world.

Appendix A

- ∅ Alternate Dimension/Alternate Universe
- ∅ Alternate History
- ∅ Alternate Reality/Parallel Universe/Multiverse
- ∅ Fantasy
- ∅ Science Fiction
- ∅ Shadow
- ∅ Virtual Reality
- ∅ Earth
- ∅ Time Travel

And, of course, there are subgenres within the categories. The types of worlds can, and often do, overlap. The key to blending two or more worlds is balance. Some elements from a fantasy world may fit well in a science fiction world, but building a world with several elements from different types of worlds will result in something grotesque and unrecognizable. Readers won't suspend their disbelief for a story that has them jumping from medieval to space to fairy rings to avatars. The writer should try to stay with a basic structure until they have built a few successful story worlds and have discovered through their own voice and writing style which elements mix well with others.

Which world to choose? The best fit for the characters, your knowledge, or your ability to research the knowledge needed, and the time period (historical, contemporary, futuristic, or a mixture through time-travel). Or, if the characters have not shown themselves yet, choose a world that is personally appealing and intriguing.

Once the type of world is determined, a proper set of blue prints can be drawn.

Please note, these are my interpretations of the story worlds and the different types of elements that comprise them.

The Alternate Dimension/Alternate Universe

An alternate dimension is a world outside the space/time of our universe. Scientists have speculated that there may be as many as eleven dimensions, including those we recognize as width, depth, height, and time. Alternate dimensions are where the experienced world builder can have fun, and the beginning world builder can experiment. These worlds are a playground for the imagination. Any type of world can be constructed in an alternate dimension, or a mixture of worlds and creatures.

In an alternate dimension, the laws of science and physics as we understand them need not apply. For example, the sun in an alternate dimension may produce a cold light. However, the laws and rules the writer establishes must be adhered to throughout the story. They cannot be changed for convenience if they conflict with a part of the plot.

The story may start in an alternate dimension with characters moving from one alternate dimension to another, or the writer can transport the characters to another dimension from Earth. Transporting characters from one alternate dimension to another takes some care, along with a source of energy with enough power to pull the characters from one dimension to another. Unfortunately, it is also more than enough power to kill the characters. It is the writer's job to set up the rules and give a plausible explanation as to why the characters were able to survive the energy. It should be so seamlessly woven into the characters, the plot, and the world that the reader's suspension of disbelief is maintained. The writer does not want the reader to stop and question the how and why of an element of the story world.

It has been suggested that dreams are also portals to an alternate dimension as they often have elements that defy the physical universe as we know it. A psychic character, or a character who has latent psychic ability, might enter an alternate dimension through a dream portal. Things to consider with this scenario are whether the character can control travel between dimensions through dreams, and whether the character can contact others who do not have psychic ability and take them through the portal by entering the other character's dreams.

Whichever mode of transport the writer decides to use, it must be logical in the confines of the story and story world.

Alternate History

An alternate history story is much more than taking a historical fact and changing it to fit a story. Cause and effect should be taken into consideration. If the Boston Tea Party had never occurred, would there still have been a Revolutionary War? These stories require a lot of research, not only of the events to be changed, but what those events affected and the results. Also, the alternate results should have a reasonable theory to justify them.

Alternate Reality/Parallel Universe/Multiverse

An alternate reality, sometimes referred to as a parallel universe, differs from an alternate dimension. Where the physical laws of science need not apply in an alternate dimension, they do apply in an alternate reality. In essence, an alternate reality or parallel universe is our world in a different timeline. Suppose Germany, or even a country that was neutral in our history, like Argentina, had won World War II. Suppose a meteor had never hit the Earth and caused the Ice Age. What if electricity had never been discovered, or penicillin? According to theory, these are realities in parallel universes. The term multiverse is used when referencing all possible scenarios to consist of all reality.

A word of caution, here. A different timeline in the sense that an event happened that wasn't supposed to happen, or an event that was supposed to happen never happened, is different than events that take place in another dimension outside the space/time of our universe. If it's 2008 when the character enters the alternate reality, it will still be 2008 in the alternate reality. The flow of time doesn't change, only the events.

The characters may start in their own reality and travel to ours, or vice-versa. However, it is the point of an alternate reality world to show the differences in the realities. Otherwise, the story is simply an alternate history story.

Fantasy

The classic sword and sorcery story, often referred to as high fantasy, is set in a world where the women are fair, the men are heroes, and the black knight or evil wizard is set on destroying them all. The fantasy world contains magic in all its forms: white magic, black magic, and earth magic, as well as alchemy. Magic is an accepted part of the everyday life in a fantasy world. However, the magic bestowed on a character through the plot often comes with a price or consequences not expected by the characters.

Life in the high fantasy world is simple with very little technology and often resembles Europe in the Middle Ages. The main characters are often called upon to perform some heroic deed, or they may be called upon to journey on a quest either to win a great prize, or to save the kingdom.

In the fantasy story world, more so than the other story worlds, the inhabitants are integral. A fantasy world will have castles, unicorns, fairies, witches, wizards, alchemists, trolls, angels, etc. These inhabitants will live, for the most part, in harmony with the human inhabitants. In contrast, dark fantasy will have vampires, demons, dragons, werewolves, gargoyles, harpies, and other assorted beasts and monsters. The tone of dark fantasy may drift to horror, and there is conflict with the human inhabitants.

The urban fantasy story world has many of the same elements of the high fantasy or dark fantasy story, only these stories take place on Earth in a contemporary setting. They are usually, but not always, shadow worlds (which are covered in a later section).

The science fiction fantasy world is based on science that is not based on any type of real science, but simply conjured by the mind of the writer. Comic book stories are a good example of science fiction fantasy, as the characters often conduct science experiments that go wrong and cause a superhero or villain when there is absolutely so scientific proof behind the outcome of the experiment.

Science Fiction

Science fiction story worlds encompass more than outer space, although planets and other outer space locations, such as space stations and asteroids are arguably the most popular. Robots, experiments with dire consequences, time travel, super computers, super plagues, and cyber and steam punk are all part of the science fiction genre. Government and religion will usually play a large role in a science fiction story as the moral issues and societal impacts brought about by the new technologies will be an underlying theme of the story.

Hard-core science-fiction aficionados want the science part to be as close to our known science as possible with reasonable postulates. The reader might allow some artistic license, but no reader will allow the author to play fast and loose with outrageous science that has absolutely no basis in fact. Those stories fall more into the fantasy world than the science fiction world.

Flying cars, space travel, time travel, transporters, sonic showers, molecular restructuring for production of food and other materials, genetics, bionics, and nanotechnology are just a few of the many elements found in science fiction works. And while not all of them are based on scientific fact, most are generally accepted in the space opera subgenre of science fiction. For instance, travel at the speed of light or faster than the speed of light is deemed to be impossible, but it has become so ingrained in the culture of the science fiction world, readers will often overlook it. But not always. It's a good idea to check and double check the guidelines of the publisher and to read some of what the house publishes before submitting to discover which science fiction elements are allowed. This is also a good idea when considering any publisher, not only those publishers who deal with speculative fiction.

And speaking of space opera, here are some common mistakes to avoid when writing a story set in space. These are just a few, and it's a good idea to do a little research on bad movie science or bad movie physics. These critics of movie science can give great insight as to what signifies as good, bad, and indifferent science mistakes. As a matter of course, do a little research on any type of technology when contemplating its use in a story.

> ✄ There is no air or oxygen in space; it is a vacuum. Therefore sound does not travel and there are no flames. So, when the hero is on the deck of his ship and has launched the fatal attack, he will not hear the explosion of the enemy ship, nor will he see fire or flames. Even if it was a huge enemy ship filled with oxygen, the oxygen will dissipate too quickly to burn.

However, he will see the flash from the explosion.

⌀ People and objects do not move slower in zero gravity. And a person in the center of a spin (such as to "create gravitational forces") will not feel the effects of the spin. If you want to test this, sit in the middle of a merry-go-round while it is moving.

⌀ A body will not instantly freeze or explode when exposed to the vacuum of space.

⌀ Instant communication between humans and aliens without some sort of translation device is unbelievable.

Research isn't only for the space opera subgenre. Medical issues must be researched for a super plague. Steam engines and inventions of the Victorian era, such as the Babbage engine, should be researched for steampunk, as well as the dissenters of technology, commonly known as Luddites. A writer wanting to pen a cyberpunk novel should research computer technology, and a writer interested in extinction level events should research space phenomena, volcanoes, etc.

Shadow

A shadow world is one that exists in tandem with the real world, in real world locations, but is generally unknown to the human inhabitants. Vampire stories are usually set in shadow worlds. They have their own societies and walk among the humans, but the humans have no knowledge of their existence. Except, for instance, the vampire slayer.

A skillful writer can create a shadow world with almost any type of inhabitant and use almost any of the different story worlds to create the shadow world. Fairies are often written as having their own society, as are leprechauns, aliens, and werewolves (although the pack society is much smaller than that of a fairy society).

Humans with psychic abilities also fall into the category of a shadow world. The psychic's world is functionally different from the non-psychic's. Although psychics may work, play, live, and essentially be a part of society, their world remains hidden to the other inhabitants. When you can hear other people's thoughts, or enter other people's dreams, or move objects with a thought, you tend to keep it a secret. Fear is probably the best reason to keep the secret. Fear of being labeled a witch, demon, or freak, the fear of being forced into years of testing by the government, and the threat of other people fearing you are all good reasons not to tell others of special abilities.

Of course, some characters equate their ability with fame and fortune, and they don't allow those fears into their lives. They write books, do demonstrations, and appear on late-night television talk shows. Again, this is a world far different from the everyday life.

The skill needed to write an engaging shadow world lies in the blending of the story world with the real world while keeping them segregated enough to make the ignorance of the humans plausible.

Virtual Reality

A virtual reality is a world inside the confines of a computer-generated landscape. The inhabitants are depicted as avatars inside the VR, and they may be cartoonish or realistic. The VR landscape can be entered through a private or public terminal, or through a specially made VR device, such as a chair, or a set of VR goggles.

The landscape and scenery may appear warped, as if the visitor is looking at it through thick glass, or as some form of animation. The visitor will not be allowed outside the boundaries of the VR, nor will everyone and everything inside the VR interact with the visitor. The visitor must be vigilant though, because his contact in the VR may have chosen a tree as an avatar, or a sign, or a flower. Nothing in the VR world can be overlooked or dismissed. Everyone and everything is a potential enemy or a potential source of information.

One of the considerations for the virtual reality is how much the VR world affects the character whose physical presence is still in the real world. If the character is injured or dies in the VR, will he bleed or die in the real world? If the character falls in love with another VR character, can their love be sustained in the real world?

Another consideration is addiction. Will a character become so addicted to the VR world that he doesn't disconnect to take care of basic human needs like food? And what happens if the character refuses to leave the VR world remains "plugged in" to the point where the constant stimulation doesn't allow the mind to rest. Sleep deprivation causes a reduction in problem solving, a lack of creative thinking, and other brain function problems, and can cause hallucinations if the deprivation is severe. If the character in a VR world is fighting bad guys, or seeking information, the effects of sleep deprivation can be deadly, in the real world as well as the VR world.

Earth

Earth? Yes, Earth. Perhaps a settler from another planet has colonized on Earth, or a civilization has been living at the bottom of the ocean, or deep within the mountains of Tibet, or underground beneath the harsh landscape of the tundra. A post-apocalyptic Earth, or any vision of Earth after some sort of war, plague, or natural disaster, will look and feel much different than it does now. Then there's always Atlantis, or any other mythical city that is perceived to be hidden somewhere on Earth.

Story worlds need to be built for these scenarios, with the limits of our physical world. The aliens will definitely have some technologies not yet discovered, as may the other hidden societies. However, in order to avoid detection, these societies will have a system in place for keeping their secrets hidden. They may not have any immunity built for the diseases that have developed on the surface of the planet or outside of their "protected" boundaries. They may have developed a disease for which the rest of Earth's inhabitants have no immunity. Food, clothing, dwellings, will be vastly different for the hidden societies than for the Earth as we know it.

If the inhabitants of a hidden society interact with the inhabitants of Earth, voluntarily or otherwise, they will bring pockets of their society with them. The air will be different for them, as will the taste of foods, the temperature, and for a character who has lived closer to the Earth's core, the force of gravity at the surface will feel different. All of these details should be taken into consideration.

A post-apocalyptic Earth may be contaminated by nuclear fallout, either from war or as a result from some sort of space event. A plague or epidemic may leave water, soil, and food contaminated with mutated strains of the disease from decaying bodies that were never properly buried or destroyed. Technology of the time probably won't work, either from destruction, or the lack of individuals who know how to operate it. Landscapes may be a heap of rubble, or bleak cities where only life was destroyed. Eventually, those cities left intact will become ghost towns or legends, perhaps a utopian place the characters try to find.

Time Travel

Time travel has fascinated the human race since the first person wished they could change something in their past. But if one event is changed, how does it affect the flow of time from that point forward? It is the paradox that time travel creates which fascinates us, such as "the grandfather paradox" that essentially asks, "If I go back in time and kill my grandfather before my father is born, will I exist?"

These stories can be science fiction, using postulates from known theories to effectuate the actual time travel, or they can be fantasies using magic or some other non-scientific means to achieve time travel.

The objective of the time travel can be anything. To right a wrong, to rediscover an ancient technology, to prevent or stop a war, or something as simple as sightseeing.

As with alternate history, time travel requires a bit of research, and cause and effect should be taken into consideration, especially when dealing with the time travel paradox.

Appendix B

On Earth, we have a variety of governments to use as a model for a story world. Some are recognizable and used in different parts of the world while others have long since vanished from the governmental landscape. These are very brief and broad descriptions of the governments listed on the world building worksheet.

- ☒ Anarchy
- ☒ Communism
- ☒ Democracy
- ☒ Dictatorship
- ☒ Egalitarian
- ☒ Feudalism
- ☒ Monarchy
- ☒ Oligarchy
- ☒ Republic
- ☒ Theocracy
- ☒ Totalitarian
- ☒ Tribal

Anarchy

Anarchy is a total lack of government. Think barbarism. There are no governmental controls of rules, no punishments, and no system to ensure that any task gets done for the common good. Some societies in the story world may start in anarchy or spiral down into anarchy as a result of war or some sort of natural disaster.

Communism

Communism is a form of government in which all individuals have equality. There are no officials. Each member of a communist society shares the work and the wealth. No one individual has more influence or power than another. This sort of system is appealing, but there are always complications.

Democracy

Democracy is a form of government in which the people elect the leaders. In a democratic republic, a representative is elected to represent the peoples' interests to the leaders. In theory, the representative would always cede to the majority of the individuals of the electorate. However, if an individual has more power, or money, or influence within the electorate, the representative will feel pressure to please that individual.

Dictatorship

A dictatorship is where one individual seizes and takes control of the government, usually with military force. The leader's word is final, and there is no consideration for the people of the society for which the dictator rules. Punishments are often swift, harsh, and inconsistent. Fascism is also a dictatorship that values nation or race over individual, and has strict control over economic and social structures.

Egalitarian

An egalitarian system of government declares all citizens equal in social stature, economic stature, etc., and is similar to the communist and socialism doctrines. A true egalitarian system is most often found in small governmental systems, like a village, tribe, or clan. Otherwise, giving every citizen an equal part of the whole is not feasible. Some contributions will always outweigh others, and this becomes more apparent in larger governmental systems.

Feudalism

Feudalism is a hierarchal form of government, usually royal. In return for military service, a lord grants land to a vassal, such as a knight. The vassal can then grant small parcels of his land to farmers, blacksmiths, weavers, etc. These workers give a large portion of their goods and services to the vassal, who in turn also gives a portion to the lord. It should be noted, though, that there are many different academic views of feudalism, and if a writer intends to use this system of government, a lot more research is necessary.

Monarchy

A monarchy is a form of government that revolves around royalty. A king or queen has absolute power in a monarchy. The children of the monarchs are the heirs to the power. The monarch may have advisors and will most often appoint law enforcement officials and judges to police different regions. This system of government is usually seen in high fantasy and secret societies.

Oligarchy

An oligarchy is a form of government in which the rich or elite rule. The oligarchs are usually a shadow government that controls the figure-head government such as a royal family, religious leader, or some other type. The children of the oligarchs expect to be heirs to the power.

Republic

A republic is similar to a democracy in that some or all parts of the government are representatives of the people. However, the president, chancellor, king, etc., may not hold the highest power. Those positions can be ceremonial or advisory. A counsel or consul may be the highest power in a republic. A republic is one of the hardest government systems to write, because a peoples' perception of a republic varies as to the rules of a republic, the highest authority, and the breadth of governmental control.

Theocracy

A theocracy is a form of government that is controlled by a religion. The religious leaders determine laws, punishments, acceptable behavior, etc., by the tenets of the religion.

Totalitarian

A totalitarian system of government is similar to a dictatorship. The government controls every aspect of life for its citizens. The government controls all culture, such as what television and movies may be viewed, which religion may be practiced, which books may be read, etc. It may be from a totalitarian's own sense of morality or that of a religion. Contraband is dealt with swiftly and harshly.

Tribal

A tribal or clan society is usually a close-knit society in which many of the citizens have familial ties, most often from a common ancestor or god. True familial ties need not be present, as people can be accepted into the tribe/clan by performing a service or pledging their lives to the good of the tribe/clan. The chief or laird is the highest power and usually makes decisions on crime and punishment and tribe/clan activities.

Appendix C

As with governmental systems, our own history and present day systems provides a wealth of information on which to model an economic system. Some will be more familiar than others. Here are some very brief and broad descriptions of the economic systems listed on the world-building worksheet.

- ☒ Barter
- ☒ Free Market or Capitalist
- ☒ Corporate Owned
- ☒ Planned
- ☒ Socialism
- ☒ Spoils of War
- ☒ Tribute

Barter

A barter economy is a system in which food, goods, services, or information is traded for other goods, services, food, or information. This type of economic system is often seen in young governments, or established tribal/clan governments, and some feudalistic governments. Spy networks may also establish a bartering network, no matter the systems of government they encounter.

Free Market

A free market or capitalist economy is a system based on supply and demand. Producers are free to price their products based on what the market can bear with no interference from governmental agencies. There are no set prices, no price controls, and no protections against price gouging. A weaver can sell cloth to a merchant for one price and, in the next minute, sell the same amount of cloth of the same quality to the next customer for more or less money.

Corporate Owned

A corporate-owned economy is a system in which large corporations control every aspect of goods and services sold. The corporation will own the land on which food is grown, as well as the equipment, fertilizer, storage, etc., and will pay the farmer. The corporation can then set and control the price of the food. One corporation may have many subsidiaries that own and control many different industries, or each industry may be owned and controlled by a different corporation.

Planned

A planned economy is a system in which the government has control over the goods produced and control over the prices for goods and services sold. The government may look at its citizens and determine only a certain amount of wheat is needed and either force some wheat farmers to do something else or force others to become wheat farmers. The government looks at all natural resources and determines which may be used in production, such as coal for furnaces or trains, wood for building houses, gold for currency or jewelry, etc.

Socialism

Socialism is an economic system in which the government doesn't own or control the production of goods and services, but does control the distribution of those goods and services to its citizens. This system usually goes hand-in-hand with an egalitarian system of government or a communist system of government. Every citizen is equal in voting stature, social stature, and wealth.

Spoils of War

A spoils of war economic system is common for a warrior society. The warriors may have a home base, but they are generally nomadic, traveling to their next conquest. The warriors take what they need and want from the people they conquer, sell or trade what they do not want, and may send a portion to their home base.

Tribute

A tribute economic system is similar to a spoils of war system. An invading army takes a city or region by force, but leaves as much of the infrastructure as possible. The invaders appoint positions that are filled by their countrymen, and these overseers insure that a certain amount of money, or goods and services, or both is paid in tribute to the victor. Sometimes one government will demand tribute from a weaker government prior to invading, with the promise that the weaker government will not be invaded, or with the promise that it will protect the weaker government from other invaders.

ABOUT THE AUTHOR

Award winning author TG Franklin lives in East Tennessee, and she often mines ideas from the rich and diverse cultural and scientific communities from Oak Ridge to the Smoky Mountains.

An avid science fiction fan, she spent many hours dissecting plots, characters, and technologies of the great sci-fi shows and movies of the 70s with her father over a cup of coffee at the kitchen table. Her writing reflects those early influences as well as current innovations in technology.

When she isn't writing, she loves riding her motorcycle through the Smoky Mountains, and painting.

OTHER WORKS BY TG FRANKLIN

Amethyst Nights
Sensual Energy
Imago

Essential Pre-Writing Workbook
World Building Guide & Workbook
The Creative Writer's Planner/Journal
Reading Together: A Reading Journal for Book Group Members
Reading is My Passion A Book Journal for Bibliophiles
Elder Care Journal

If you enjoyed this book, please consider leaving a review.

Printed in Great Britain
by Amazon